The Secret of
Radiant Life

W. E. SANGSTER

The Secret of Radiant Life

ABINGDON PRESS

NEW YORK NASHVILLE

THE SECRET OF RADIANT LIFE

Library of Congress Catalog Card Number: 57-9789

SET UP, PRINTED, AND BOUND BY THE PARTHENON PRESS, AT NASHVILLE, TENNESSEE, UNITED STATES OF AMERICA

PREFACE

Many people find life disappointing. They are haunted by the feeling that it ought to be inwardly satisfying, and that if it were so it would be outwardly radiant. But nothing deeply satisfies them for long, and they have never lost themselves in some great cause large enough for whole-life dedication. Even when material circumstances are kindly, they still go about wanting something more, and not a few are reading books on how to be happy.

Many writers have tried to help them. Some concentrate on the physical basis of human existence and write on vitamins. Others are sure that it all depends on "how you think." I am of those who are quite certain that the basic answer is a spiritual one. I would not presume to deny the relevance of physical and mental factors. With so much of the East hungry, who can be indifferent to vitamins? With a third of the hospital beds in the Western world occupied by people mentally or nervously ill, who can be anything but grateful to those who minister to minds diseased? But neither a full stomach nor a clear mind takes the ache from human hearts. Man was made for God. All parts of our personality are drawn to health when he is resident within. Certain as many people are that religion is just a matter of taste and life can be satisfying without it, I am sure that they are mistaken and that those who refuse to consider the claims of the spiritual shut themselves out from the fulfillment they seek. This book begins with the deep conviction that our healing and wholeness are in God.

But it begins also with the conviction that it isn't easy to make that fact clear. Apart from the difficulties of explaining it, so many of us Christians are poor examples. We are not *all* inwardly content nor outwardly radiant. Many people who are regular at church are as fretful and anxious as their church-neglecting neighbors. I had, therefore, in writing this book, two groups of people in mind: people outside the Church who find life disappointing but are willing to read a book which is frankly religious, and those inside the Church who (in their moments of starkest honesty) are willing to admit that religion has never come alive for them and loyalty more than conviction keeps them linked with the Church at all. I begin with the belief that all normal people desire peace of mind and covet also that sparkle on the personality which inward peace naturally brings . . . and I move on from there.

I have written for plain people and avoided any parade of scholarship. To be as simple and practical as possible has been my aim throughout.

Even so, my central conviction that this deep hunger of the human soul can only be satisfied when God is resident within the heart will seem mystical and "airy-fairy" to many. All talk of the life of God in the soul of man appears a difficult idea for some to entertain and remotely far from practical life.

Yet I have essayed that difficult task and I will have at least the sympathy of those other teachers who are working in this same segment of the field. Many are saying in their own accent what I am seeking to say here.

It all centers in Christ. In him we see the life we can have. In him we see the men and women we now are. He is himself the way from the one to the other.

In my efforts to be practical I have even given exercises or meditations. I make no claim to have pressed far down this path, but I am certain that it is the right one.

My warmest thanks are due to my one-time colleague, the Rev. T. C. Baird, who kindly read the typescript, and to Mrs. Timmons and Miss Leonora McCroft, who prepared it from my manuscript.

Westminster

W. E. SANGSTER

CONTENTS

PART ONE

THE LIFE

The Person I Could Be

PART TWO

THE TRUTH

The Person I Am

PART THREE

THE WAY

The Path Between

PART ONE

THE LIFE

The Person I Could Be

1

WE WANT TO BE RADIANT PERSONALITIES

Every normal person would like to be a radiant personality: to be respected, attractive, and, indeed, loved; to be at peace within, useful, happy, and sought after—not just for the things he might be able to give, but for himself alone.

If there are people who deny all this and say that they do not care a bit what others think of them, and even seem to enjoy being disagreeable, that is only a proof that they are odd. Some mishandling in childhood or some major defeat in later life has given them a kink, and it is not less a kink because they have come to take pride in it. We are so made that we cannot hate our kind and be happy ourselves, and people who seem to get pleasure from being unpleasant are twisted in their thinking and emotionally immature.

Any *normal* person wants to be at peace with himself and in happy and easy relations with others, and to anybody possessing this inner treasure something else is added: an outward sparkle on his personality or at least the glow of a quiet joy. If he is young, it shows itself in an infectious gaiety; if he is in the middle years, it may be less ebullient, but it is even more appealing because it is more rare. In old age, it seems loveliest of all; it fulfills all that Wordsworth wished:

> . . . an old age, serene and bright
> And lovely as a Lapland night.

But how does one get it? What is the way to radiant personality?

Some people think that this glowing attitude toward life turns entirely on *health*—by which they mean plain physical fitness. That health has its part to play none will deny, but to reduce the whole question to physical fitness ignores the close interrelation of mind and body and grossly oversimplifies the whole thing. Any doctor with a large practice will tell you that he has patients who are physically sound (though they will not long remain that way!) but who are miserable, repellent, and sick of life. Any minister with a large church will tell you that he knows people who are bedfast but bright with a light which seems not of this earth.

Some people think that it is all a matter of *"temperament"*—whatever they mean by that vague word. The Greeks had a theory that each person is born with a certain cast of mind and that this remains practically unmodified throughout life. The four chief forms, they said, are the sanguine, phlegmatic, choleric, and melancholic. Now (say some modern theorists), each of us is in one or another of those categories . . . and we can do nothing about it. These people with "radiant personalities" belong to the first group. They were *born* bright. If you are in one of the other groups, well—that is a pity, but it must be endured. You will be unemotional, hot-tempered, or inclined to misery until you die.

One does not deny the grain of truth which lies in this talk about temperament when one emphatically denies the suggestion that it explains all life. You need not be a prisoner of your inheritance. Millions of men and women have been made free. The phlegmatic sparkle; the choleric are urbane; the melancholic bubble with joy. There is a power abroad in the universe greater than temperament. You, also, can be gay.

Still others explain the presence or absence of radiancy in life by *circumstances*. "It all depends on environment," they say. "If you have a nice home, an adequate income, a wide circle of dependable friends, congenial work, and good health, you can be happy; lacking these things, you cannot. It all depends on *things*."

But life does not confirm this view. I have just read in the paper of the suicide of a lady who had a lovely home, a more than ample income, a wide circle of dependable friends, and (on the assurance of her doctor at the inquest) excellent health. But she *thought* she was ill. People who have all the *things* which others say are necessary to happiness often lack happiness. Others, without those things, unconsciously shine as though they were alight within.

Nor do they long remain in lack of most of those other desirable things. Happiness draws friendship: people like to be with the happy.

Happiness is an enemy to sickness: it can drive out many forms of sickness by itself alone. The radiant life is no more determined by circumstances than it is by fitness or temperament. It *molds* all three, but it is not subject to them. The great and open secret must be sought elsewhere.

Heavy sorrows and severe testings come to all men and women who live for any length of days, and nobody can come home smiling from the grave of his dearest. But it is possible, even then, to come home in inward *peace.*

Moreover, the great sorrows of life by their very nature cannot come frequently, and there is comfort to be found in hours as dark as these.

You can be a radiant personality. The determining factors are externally fixed. Indeed, everything that is externally *fixed* is fixed for your advantage.

During the war I was talking one day with a group of men in a large room when a friend of mine entered at the further end. My friend is a radiant personality. The conversation around me turned to him.

"That fellow always seems to be getting a kick out of life," one man remarked.

"He does," said the medical man in our company—and laughed. "What a fine liver he must have!"

"He has no worries, I expect," said another member of the party. "I don't suppose *he's* got a boy at the war."

"He's probably having a very good time in business," said somebody else, "making a pile."

One by one they explained my friend's mastery of life. Finally I broke in. I knew him with an intimacy none of the rest shared.

"Well, he has reasonably good health," I admitted. "But he's not making a pile! He's a schoolmaster. No! He has no boy at the war. In fact, he has three children. One is normal; one is deaf and dumb; and his only son is deaf, dumb, and an idiot. If you want to explain that man's fine quality of life, you must look elsewhere."

And that is what *we* must do.

Physical fitness, temperament, and circumstances are not prime causes and do not of themselves explain radiant personality.

For the secret spring of that, we must look elsewhere.

TO SUM UP

All normal people would like to be attractive personalities.

All *can* be.

It is not finally determined by

health,
temperament,
circumstances.

You can have radiance too.

2

BUT IT IS NOT A HUMAN ACHIEVEMENT

No one can achieve radiant personality alone.

If some people find that assertion disappointing, it is at least direct and honest. Human effort alone is unequal to this. The long history of our race proves it.

Convinced (as we have seen) that the whole secret is in a sound body, some people make a proper concern for physical fitness into a fetish and carry the study of vitamins and exercises to obsessional length. Yet many of them do not even know what they are keeping fit *for!*

Still others (as we noticed) put the whole stress upon circumstances and try to mold the details of life "nearer to the heart's desire." Men toil for money in the big city and often wreck their health with their endeavors, and then move to the country because they think the country is more conducive to peace. Many of them are chasing a will-o'-the-wisp. They have a hunger in them for total security. They seek a kind of fortress in which they can live untouched by the chances and changes of this mortal life—a place inviolate from all disaster and subject to variation only as it is subject to growth and greater peace. Few figures are more pathetic than that of the retired man in comfortable circumstances, with his money wisely invested against an economic blizzard (from whichever quarter it might come), sitting in his lovely garden with an awful fear in his heart that things "won't stay put," and reading a book on "how to be happy."

Nor do fame and position seem to yield that deep content. If one may judge by the comments of those who have achieved it, one soon gets used to the fame and may even find it unpleasantly intrusive at times. As for position, nothing seems permanent. The younger men tread on your heels. A man can still feel young himself when those younger are overheard to wonder "when that old fellow will get out of the way" and when those who defend him do so with reservations: "But he's wonderful *for his age.*"

The people who think that inner peace and radiant personality depend primarily on fitness, fame, and fortune had better think again.

Still others have persuaded themselves that the secret of happiness and the glowing life is "inside them"—and inside all other men and women too. They put a shallow interpretation on a deep word of Jesus Christ and say: "The kingdom of heaven is within you." After that, many of them have little more to say about Jesus. But they go on insisting that the secret is "within"!

If the secret of victorious living is already in the human heart, it must have got seriously overlaid.

Put the matter to a simple test! Stand at a busy street corner for ten minutes and study the faces of the people who go by. Or sit in a train and observe unobtrusively the expressions of your fellow passengers. How few look happy! How seldom a face in repose is a face of serene content. The kingdom of heaven within them! As they are? The obvious falsity of it should have convinced all who respect Jesus of Nazareth that he meant something deeper than that.

Still others are convinced that the secret of interior joy and radiant living depends on how you think—which is a discerning and important part of the truth. But only a part! People who offer this teaching talk much about "laws"—as though law was a great force in itself and all you have to do is to "open yourself" to certain benign laws.

But law is not a force in itself; it is a form. It is not creative but descriptive. It is not operative but directive. The great Life behind and within the universe cuts its own channels, and *we* call them "laws."

And the great Life behind and within the universe is the life of God.

However distasteful some people may find it, there is no way to the mastery of life and to radiant personality which leaves out God. He made us and he made us for himself. Augustine said some fifteen hundred years ago on the first page of his famous *Confessions:* "Thou hast made us for Thyself, and our heart is restless till it finds rest in Thee."

Something stubborn in man resists this inescapable and sublime fact. Usually it is pride. Pride prevents our asking forgiveness for the wrongs we know we have done. Pride tells us that we are too intelligent to believe in God! Pride persuades us that we belong to ourselves and that the dignity (!) of human personality prevents our submitting to anybody else. Fear adds its quota too. The fear of submission. The fear of the consequences. The fear of our own soiled pasts.

So we will look anywhere for peace and joy—except where alone it can be found. So—even when we are half-convinced that the quest is useless—we still search for it in the wrong places. Pride and perversity stiffen our spirits, and some will press on to certain disappointment rather than bow the knee to the God who made us.

Perhaps where preachers have failed to persuade people, psychologists may succeed. Carl Jung, the eminent psychologist, said:

> During the past thirty years, people from all the civilized countries of the earth have consulted me. . . . Among all my patients in the second half of life—that is to say, over thirty-five—there has not been one whose problem in the last resort was not that of finding a religious outlook on life. It is safe to say that every one of them fell ill because he had lost that which the living religions of every age have given to their followers, and none of them has been really healed who did not regain his religious outlook.

We need God! There is the truth of it. The demands of our turbulent nature are not to be calmed and controlled by the human will alone. The stupid purposelessness of a universe without meaning sickens us in the very soul. The vanity of still supposing that our race can *save itself* from destruction even while we drift to the things we dread is a conceit we can no longer entertain. The ache for inward peace and the outward sheen which betokens its presence are not made on this earth.

We turn to God.

"Help us, O God!"

Where the saints and seers of all the ages have found victory and peace, we will find it too.

TO SUM UP

No man can make himself a radiant personality.
Fame and fortune cannot secure it.
Nor is it already "within."
Nor is it just the fruit of thinking.
It is a gift of God.

3

IT IS A GIFT OF GOD

THE idea that radiant personality is a gift of God is difficult for some people to receive. "Even assuming the existence of a supreme being," they say, "is it likely that his concerns would descend to details, and that it would matter to him whether earth-born creatures were radiant personalities or not? With a universe to manage, and multitudes to feed, and the high statesmanship of Deity to direct, can we even conceive that he would have a personal watch over individuals:

In teeming millions can He care,
Can special love be everywhere?

The very idea of it seems ludicrous, and men brush it aside.

It is well that we be reminded of our littleness in the universe. There is something of selfishness and vanity in those people who (ignoring the greater needs of others) suppose that the important business of God in every day is to keep them bright! Radiant personality, as we shall learn later, is a by-product. People who deliberately set out for it and make it their supreme end in living will miss it. They must! Selfishness is self-defeating. Selfishness is still selfishness, even when it is a good thing which you are seeking. The sin of selfishness is not found in the end pursued (for that might be a noble virtue!) but in the fact that *you* are living for yourself *alone*. The main motive of my life becomes what *I* want. Life resolves itself into "Give me! Give me! Give me!"—and an absorbing concern with oneself is the certain way to spiritual debility and the end of all hope of radiant life.

So the paradoxical truth is this: that if you want to be a radiant personality you had better forget about it. It is when (as we shall see) something else rather wonderful happens that radiant personality comes in on the side. It is like the bloom of perfect health. The bloom comes of itself and charms us as the unconscious revelation of something deeper. People try to fake radiance sometimes, and go about with a spurious geniality which is unrelated to anything inside. It is like the dab of rouge on the face of a sick woman. It means nothing. Indeed, it lies!

But while it is good that each one of us be reminded that he is not the only person in the universe, it is important that we be reminded also that we *are* persons and dear, in our individuality, to God. Almost all the higher religions teach the value of human personality, but Christianity teaches it most clearly of all. Christ said that God cares so much for his created universe that a sparrow cannot fall unnoticed to the earth. Then he added (as he looked on the poor people standing about him): "You are of more value than many sparrows." (R.S.V.) He said something else also. To leave them in no doubt that God's care descends to details, he used the most extravagant metaphor that was at hand. He said with a smile: *"The very hairs of your head are all numbered."*

To everyone for whom the word of Christ has supreme authority, that is settled forever. God loves us deeply and personally, and there is not a detail of our lives of unconcern to him. There are things about life we would like to have known, but Christ never told us. But he told us that God's watchful care is over every one of us—and everything else is given with that. If God is there and cares as much as that, *nothing else ultimately matters.* Cancer, earthquakes, famine, floods . . . all the ugly God-denying phenomena with which our world is darkened will be explained. There is a friend behind phenomena —indeed, a *Father* behind it all; and in the hollow of his hand we have our being. Give him the wide margin of eternity and he will justify his ways with men. He is great enough to maintain his universe and take a father's care of his child.

I noticed in the newspapers the other day that some letters from his wife (Marie Louise) to Napoleon had been offered for sale. Some people seemed amused at the triviality of their contents. They were mostly about their little son. He had had the toothache. The toothache was better. He had been in bed a few days. He was up again now. . . . "What letters to write," some commentators said, "to a man on the battlefield engaged in world conquest!"

But what else *could* she have written? What else did he *want* her to write? Does a general cease to be a father, and an emperor cease to love his son?

And the deeper cosmic truth is this: that the Ruler of the universe is our Father—even though millions are ignorant of the fact and many, though half aware of it, are estranged from him—and, being our Father, he watches over us with paternal care and aches to give us all good things.

He has nothing more precious to give than his peace, and those who have his peace "shine forth as the sun." No one should be ashamed of longing to possess it.

"But ought we to *want* peace in a world as troubled as this?" some people ask. "The threat of dreadful war hangs over us. Millions starve. Multitudes are homeless. Women sell their bodies for bread. . . . Is it right even to *covet* peace and radiant personality in a world as foul as this?"

It is right—and natural too! It is a reminiscence in the soul of our Creator's intention for us. He crowns all his other gifts with the gift of peace, and wherever there is God's peace, there is radiance.

Moreover, he extends his rule among men by this means. The radiant life is the attractive life. Men marvel—and inquire! Nothing moves people more to reach out for the life of God than the vision of it in some soul filled with his peace and shining with joy. Even the worldly wonder. They fancy themselves specialists in enjoying themselves, but they feel in their souls that they have no joy like this. They spend their days pointing to tainted pleasures and urging young people to "see life," but here is shining life of a quality they had not even dreamed.

So—by living examples—God put a thirst in the souls of those least likely to turn to him. If all who profess and call themselves Christians had this quality of life, the tide of God would come in as a flood. It would be clear in the gaze of all the people that "our God is marching on."

You are not wrong to want radiant personality. You must just understand clearly how it comes.

TO SUM UP

Some people find it hard to believe that God cares for individuals and would give them peace and radiant life.

Yet he does! He is great enough to maintain his universe and take a father's care of his child.

But ought we even to *want* peace and radiance in a world as dark as this?

We are not wrong to want it.

We are only wrong to forget that it is a by-product and waits on a wonderful "something else."

4

IT IS THE GIFT OF GOD HIMSELF

What is this wonderful "something else" of which the radiant life is but the outward expression?

Incredible though it will seem to an irreligious man, God (the great God of the universe) will come by invitation and live in any man's life. Live in him: think and feel and will in his consenting servant; take up his permanent abode in that unwithdrawn life, so that (in a sense) the man may die to himself and God alone live in him. If this seems almost madness to some who read this, they must remember that it is the only explanation of the unearthly lives of the saints, and the only explanation of the miracles they performed. *Proven* miracles! Müller never asked a soul for a sou, but God gave him a million pounds to feed orphans. Catherine Booth and her husband could barely pay the rent, but they raised a mighty army which is still marching round the world. The Sadhu Sundar Singh, on his Lord's errands, crossed the oceans without money and played with the wild leopards of the jungles as though they were cats. Fantastic and indeed impossible as it may seem to many, the eternal God will make a home in a mortal heart. That is what you are asked to believe—and that is what you are invited to experience.

Sometimes those who enjoy this incredible experience are satisfied adoringly to say that God "indwells" them. Others say, "Christ lives in me." Still others call it "the infilling of the Holy Spirit." There are senses in which the difference in phrasing is quite unimportant. To the Christian it is all "the life of God in the soul of man," and no one has ever been able clearly to distinguish *in experience* among the indwelling of the Father, the Son, and the Holy Spirit. Perhaps we were never meant to. Certainly, for our purposes, the distinction need not even be discussed.

Yet there are important reasons why it will help us to think of the divine indwelling in terms of the Son. The Christian church has always believed that Christ was God in human form. He is "the image of the invisible God." He said himself: "I and the Father are one." (A.S.V., R.S.V.) His name was Immanuel—*God with us.* In Jesus, heaven came to earth. So far as humanity could express it (and clearly humanity cannot express *all* Deity), he is "all divine." And yet man!

> Our God contracted to a span
> Incomprehensibly made man.

We draw *nearer* to God in Jesus. So far as mortals can, we know him. He lived our life and bore our trials. We see him in a human setting, hear his words, and imaginatively share his experiences.

Of the Father we say:

> Beneath Thy feet we lie afar,
> And see but shadows of Thy face.

Of the Spirit we sing:

> He came in tongues of living flame,
> To teach, convince, subdue;
> All-powerful as the wind He came,
> As viewless, too.

But God is not "viewless" in Jesus—and we see more than the shadows of his face.

Jesus is God *with* us, and—in seeking to understand how God can be *in* us—it will help us to think of the great triune God in terms of the divine Son.

Here is the heart of this incredible truth which, once experienced, makes all things new and which is the whole secret of radiant personality in a phrase: God can, and will at our invitation, live in us; and those in whom God dwells (and they alone) are radiant personalities. The radiance is the outward glow of the indwelling God. It is what happens to people who really say to God, "Abide with me," and mean it, who meet his terms, who do not hinder his entrance, and who ever with gladness entertain their holy Guest. A light comes about them. They may be quite ordinary people by nature and spend all their lives doing ordinary things. But they do them in extraordinary ways. Their features may be unimpressive and indeed somber—as were the features of John Patterson Struthers, of whom people said they had never seen a face "so lustered" and on whose countenance "an amazing light would glow."

How clear it is, then, that to pursue radiant personality by itself, or for itself, is foolish. As well reach for the bloom on the peach—without the peach and without the tree! People who want the appearance of radiance without the reality must turn elsewhere. The women might take an advanced course in cosmetics . . . but it washes off! Men seeking a spurious sense of well-being and the release of their feeble wit usually look for it in a bottle . . . but there is always the "hang-over"! Even the more thoughtful methods (if they leave out God) are doomed to disappointment. The way we think—as we shall see—is immensely important, but mental gymnastics are not enough. Our thinking is but the hand which releases the spring blind; it is God's sun which pours through. Our thinking is but the touch on the guy rope, turning the canvas to the breeze; it is God's wind which fills the sail. Our thinking just turns our yearning soul in his direction; it is God himself who comes in.

Here is the thing to grasp! Difficult as the idea may be for a plain man to believe, the indwelling of Christ in the human heart is a glorious reality, enjoyed (in varying degrees) by millions, and not impossible to any human soul. It may sound mystic, occult, and impractical. But it is real, homely, and "day to day." It is for *all* men and women, in all walks of life: for cabinet ministers and cabinet makers; ambassadors and bus drivers; journalists and junior clerks. You can run a business on it, and run a home. It is *not* "airy-fairy." I can make it real, I believe, to anyone with the patience to read to the end. It is the open secret of the Christian message and leads to the finest experience this earth affords.

But let us look at it, first, in the life of a busy, practical man who was among the earliest to enjoy it.

Let us turn to the strange case of Saul of Tarsus.

TO SUM UP

God is able and willing to live in the life of any mortal who truly desires him.

Radiant personality is the glow of that divine indwelling.

To have God within us is the sublime "something else" without which peace and radiance cannot come.

It is not occult or impractical, but plain, real, and possible for all men.

5

A MAN WHO RECEIVED THE GIFT

SAUL of Tarsus was a highly gifted man. No one has ever claimed that he was among the world's great philosophers, but it is freely allowed that he had a comprehensive and keen mind. He was, moreover, singularly fortunate in his birth and circumstances. He was born into the intellectual aristocracy of the Jewish people (and was taught by their ablest scholars, becoming deeply versed in their law); but he was born and grew up in a university city of the *gentile* world and enjoyed the distinction of being a Roman citizen with easy access to the high classical learning of pagan society. Two cultures converged on this fortunate man. He seemed destined to high service in church or state.

He was, however (while still young), a deeply dissatisfied and unhappy man. Acknowledging the just claim upon him of the high moral code of his people and bending his whole strength to the fulfillment of what the moral law required, he was inwardly beaten. He sowed no wild oats and could declare without hypocrisy that he was "blameless" before the law, but he was always struggling within. He had no constant victory over his thoughts. Burning and sometimes lustful desires leaped up in him, and if he could normally prevent them from becoming deeds, he could not avoid identifying himself with those desires; and therein, as he came to believe, was the essence of sin. Nor was his will any more victorious than his thought and feeling. He would make up his mind quite resolutely not to do a certain thing . . . and then do it. He said himself: "My own behavior baffles me. I find myself not doing what I really want to do but doing what I really loathe. . . . I often find I have the will to do good, but not the power." Month after month he struggled on, but found life almost a purgatory. Time and time again he felt so utterly wretched that he almost wished his life away.

Then, in the midst of his wretchedness, something came along to distract him. A number of ignorant people had begun blasphemously to assert in Jerusalem and elsewhere that the Messiah had come. Indeed, they seemed to imply that their hero was not just God's messenger but God's Son, even God himself.

Saul had heard of this Jesus of Nazareth before. Strange stories had been in circulation of his miracle-working power. The man was a carpenter. Well! . . . a carpenter is as good as a tentmaker, of course, which was a practical craft Saul himself had mastered. Saul could not quarrel with the man's artisan status, but the fellow was completely uneducated. He had never sat in a scribal college. He had never been to a rabbinical school. He spoke with a Galilean accent and was quite untraveled. The thing had to be stamped on, of course, and the man had, very properly, been put to death.

But—here was the next incredibility!—three days after his execution, more and stranger rumors were flying around. People were saying that this Jesus had come back from the dead, and seven weeks later his followers came right out into the open and publicly proclaimed him as the Lord's Messiah, the promised one of Israel, him for whom the seers had strained their eyes through seven centuries.

It was too much! Saul offered himself immediately to the authorities (it was a blessed distraction from his own inward defeats) and flung himself fervently into the movement which aimed to stamp these Nazarenes out.

Then the greatest incredibility of all occurred! Hurtling along the road to Damascus with the resolute will and the necessary authority to root out the little group of Nazarenes in that city, Saul had the experience which altered all his life. It was noon and he had nearly reached the city when there suddenly shone around him a light brighter than the sun. It was so sudden and dazzling that he pitched to the ground, blinded by the brilliance, and heard a voice saying to him in Hebrew: "Saul, Saul, why do you persecute me?" Half-stunned as he was and lying on the ground, he could only say, "Who are you?" and the voice replied, "I am Jesus, whom you are persecuting. Go into the city. You will receive further instructions." The people with him heard the voice but did not see anyone. Saul staggered to his feet, and as his eyes were wide open, his friends did not realize at first that he could not see; but as he fumbled about, they knew his sight was gone and took him by the hands and led him into Damascus.

This experience (and deep brooding upon it) entirely changed Saul. He was utterly certain now that the crucified Nazarene was alive. It made Saul another person. He even changed his name to Paul. He was completely convinced that Jesus was indeed the Messiah, the promised one of Israel, God's only begotten Son, coequal and co-eternal with the Father, the Name at which every knee should bow.

In a comparatively short time he became a towering figure among the early Christians. Better educated than the original disciples and deeply read in Jewish law, he could explain things which still baffled them. Their preaching was mostly of the Resurrection. He saw more plainly than they did into the mystery of the Crucifixion. They exulted in the empty tomb. He rejoiced in the Resurrection too, but he wrestled with the dark enigma of the Cross and showed, more clearly than others, why the Christ had to suffer. Almost half the books of the New Testament are from his pen or by his dictation. Indeed, so immense was his influence that some people have mistakenly suggested that he altered the gospel message as Jesus left it and recast the faith in a mold of his own. Careful study does not sustain this view, but the fact that honest men have held the opinion is a further proof of the dominating influence of Paul in the early church.

But here is the fact which most concerns us now! Not only did Paul discover on the Damascus road that Christ was alive, but he also discovered that the living Christ is able and willing to live in the lives of any who would give themselves to him. The Damascus experience was over—perhaps in less than half an hour—and nothing *quite* the same ever happened to Paul again. What was *not* over, and what grew on him through the months and through the years—in freedom and captivity, on land and at sea, in success and in failure, in youth and old age—was the wonderful realization that the same Lord was not only *with* him but *in* him, thinking, feeling, and willing in the life of his obedient servant. Of all Paul's many discoveries none was more wonderful than this. Indeed, it seemed the sum of all the rest. Whatever Jesus was and is, he still is at any moment of time and right at the heart of those who bid him welcome.

It is not hard to see what this meant for Paul! That old wretchedness was gone—that dreadful weariness born of self-effort and constant defeat, that seesaw life of alternating failure and success. Previously he was constantly failing in his thinking, feeling, willing—now he had a steady success. With Christ living in him, his thoughts were pure. Temptations still assaulted him (did they not constantly assault his Master?), but as he was now strong in the strength of his resident Lord, they could not pass his moral guard. With Christ living in him, his feelings were loving. Hate and lust might suddenly flare up from his subconscious—but they would as quickly die down. They had no fuel in a heart filled full of holy love. With Christ living in him, his will was unconquerable. The things his Lord wanted him to do, he did. Indeed, they did them together. He said: "I can do all things—*in Christ*."

Paul never completely lost a sense of deep indebtedness to his old religion (he was in debt to it to the end), but it had failed him in the central moral struggle of his life; and where Judaism failed, the living and indwelling Christ succeeded. At the wonder of having Christ within him, Paul never ceased to marvel and adore.

Consider this astonishing fact! Only thirteen of Paul's letters are preserved to us. Many of them are quite short. One is barely half a page. Yet in that little sheaf of precious letters this myriad-minded man, with many, many important things to say, says one thing over and over and over again. In Christ! *In Christ!* IN CHRIST! Adolf Deissmann, the eminent German scholar, has counted the number of times Paul uses this expression—and its sister phrases ("in him," "in the Lord"). He found that it came to 164. Think!—164 times in thirteen letters, only one of which could be called long. How important it must have seemed to him! It was the key of all he had to say. The victorious life or—as we are saying here—the radiant life is the life that is lived in him. That is how one becomes "a new creature." Paul said himself: "If any man is in Christ, he is a new creature." (A.S.V.) And this is what is meant, also, by being "born again."

But I realize that some people will still think that all this talk of being "in Christ" or having Christ "in" us is mystical and unreal. They may even say that Paul, being a moral genius and spiritually unusual, is not to be regarded as a model for normal men and women.

No doubt he *was* a spiritual genius. No doubt he was a "mystic"—

in the deepest sense of the word. He had experiences ordinary people do not have and need not expect. Occasionally he had visions and revelations so unusual that he did not care to speak of them, and on the one occasion in his correspondence when he did mention such a vision, it was fourteen years after the event had occurred. Experiences like that may be called "mystical" and come only to the few. Paul never suggested that *they* were for all men.

But when he wrote and spoke of being "in Christ," he was not speaking of some rare transporting rapture possible only to people with peculiar gifts. This is for every man and woman—you and me; the butcher, the baker, the candlestick-maker . . . . *All* may be "in Christ!" All *must* be! The Christian life on any lower level is lower than the New Testament teaches as normal. One has not come to the heart of our most holy faith till one is there. Without this, the secret of the saints is hidden from us. Not as a peculiar mystic, but as a pattern we may all study and an example we may all emulate, Paul confessed one day: "I have been crucified with Christ; yet I live—and yet no longer I, but Christ lives in me."

Christ lives in me! That is the secret of radiant living. Not just Christ as my "Friend, companion, help, and guide"—precious and true as all those terms unquestionably are. But Christ *in* me.

William Law, that deep sage of the eighteenth century, said: *"A Christ not in us is a Christ not ours."*

I used to know a man who thought that he had discovered a cure for rheumatism. Certainly he got better of rheumatism himself, and people who had seen him for years creeping about in pain naturally wanted to know what had made him well. He told them gladly, gave his prescription away with cheerfulness—but then noticed that people to whom he gave the prescription often had their rheumatism still.

So he made inquiries and was astonished to learn that many people who had pestered him for the prescription had not taken the medicine when they knew what it was. They had never tried the cure inside them.

And after that, whenever he gave his prescription away, he typed in capital letters on the top of the paper: "This will do you no good —*unless you take it.*"

Christ outside us is not enough. An occasional church service and a word or nod to God are pitifully inadequate. Even regular worship, if it is only formal and perfunctory, cannot be the means of effecting the change we need. It cannot revolutionize character and produce a radiant life.

We need Christ *in* us, living at the center of our being, thinking, feeling, and willing within our eager hearts.

But how?

TO SUM UP

Saul of Tarsus was changed from a bitter persecutor into an ardent apostle by the revelation that Christ was alive and was all He said He was.

He discovered also that Christ could live in the life of any man or woman who welcomed him and could change that whole life—and keep it changed.

He called it being "in Christ," and it is the ceaseless theme of all his writing.

It is also the timeless secret of radiant personality.

But HOW does it happen?

6

GETTING READY FOR IT OURSELVES

HUMAN personality is made up of thought, feeling, and will. Whatever we mean by that elusive word "person," we mean someone who can think and feel and act. If Christ is to come into our lives, it is into all three parts that he must come.

But while we can *think* of the three parts of human personality separately, they are never really separate in experience. At different times different parts of our personality may be uppermost, but all are always present. The deepest philosopher is never only "thinking." The most ardent lover is never only "feeling." All three parts of our personality mingle, and there is a constant interaction between them.

We know that is so by the common words we use. We sometimes speak of our "attitude" toward a certain thing or another person. Our attitudes are *most* important. They regulate largely the influence we exert on others and our own openness or resistance to their influence on us. But when we come to examine what an "attitude" is, we find at once that it is a compound of thought, feeling, and will. We think certain things about that person (or thing), entertain certain feelings about him too, and have a fairly settled will toward him. All parts of our personality, therefore, are involved in our "attitude."

Or sometimes we say that we have a "mind" to do a certain thing, and though we have used the word "mind," we do not mean only a thought about it. To have a "mind" toward a certain thing means that we *feel* something about it and have a *will* toward it as well as a thought concerning it.

In considering, therefore, how Christ can come into our human personality, we must remember that he must come into thought, feeling, and will—and not into any one of them in isolation and not into all three of them *in turn*. It is into the wholeness of our personality that he must come, and steadily into all parts of our nature together.

Some people think that Christ can only come into our feelings and our will when he has been *proved* to our thought. *"Prove* him to me," they say earnestly, and seem to think that he can be "proved" only by logic or on a laboratory bench. They appear to believe that they are disloyal to reason if they profess to love Someone whose existence has not been "proved" to them, or to "give" themselves to Someone before the mind is convinced that he is there.

The mistake that they are making is to suppose that logic and the laboratory bench are the only ways to firm knowledge. We know many things unproved (and unprovable) in logic and quite incapable of demonstration on a laboratory bench. Some things we know by intuition and need no one to tell us; that kindness, for example, is better than cruelty, and the truth than a lie.

Some things we know by experience: that our mother loved us and that there was a warm security in her love. Indeed, the only way to know other persons is not by logic or test tubes, but by experience and fellowship. If a man were unwilling to make any venture into fellowship at all, he would cut himself off from some kinds of knowledge forever.

And if that is the way to know human persons and to open our lives to their influence, should it surprise us if that is the way to know the greatest Person of all?

It is like swimming. No one ever learned to swim by theory alone. When it had all been explained and demonstrated—and then explained and demonstrated again—the time came when the pupil just *had* to get into the water and trust himself to its supporting power. *There was no other way to knowledge.* It could not be proved without the personal experiment. The mother who said that her little son was never going swimming until he knew "how" was talking nonsense. Trusting the water is a necessary part of knowing how. Trusting the water is a necessary act; you have cut yourself off from that kind of certainty. Say: "No! I won't have knowledge that way"—and that means that you cannot have knowledge of those things at all.

So it is with the beginning of knowing God in any human mind. It cannot all be proved to the thought first before feeling is allowed to rise or the will to move. It is not that kind of knowing. It is the knowledge of person and Person; it involves give and take, first one and then the Other . . . and, because one person is being taught and the other is the Teacher, it involves obedience too. Christ said (on this very point): "He that does the will shall know the doctrine." DO and KNOW. Just like swimming! Get into the water and prove it. You cannot just *think* your way in. You must also *obey* your way in.

So thought, feeling, and will move together, and into that wholeness of personality Christ can come.

And it is not as though nobody ever went swimming before you! Men were swimming in the dim dawn of human history, and in the dawn of human history men were communing with the Divine. Men are not natural atheists. The natural man is inwardly aware of God. Men argue themselves into atheism, sometimes for very shabby reasons. There are those, it is true, who have come to deny the existence and goodness of God on intellectual grounds alone and must be respected; but many who deny God's existence are using "intellectual doubts" as a screen for moral failure. They do not *want* to believe in the existence of a righteous God. The memory of past wrongdoing, and sometimes their present way of life, makes it highly uncomfortable to believe that there is a righteous Judge in all the earth. So their wills move against believing, and they look around for "reasons" to bolster their unbelief. But again and again that sense that there is Someone beyond stirs in them, and they must fight to maintain the lie in their soul.

For nearly two thousand years Christ has been coming into the lives of men and women and transforming them. It is not as though you were the first person to make this experiment. Some of the first to receive him were fornicators, adulterers, perverts, thieves, swindlers, drunkards, and foul-mouthed people . . . and he made them into saints! He has been doing it in every age since. He is the supreme Specialist in making radiant personalities—but the radiance is just the outer glow of his residence within them. God is Light, and those in whom God lives, live in light.

So you are invited to venture! Even a little venture is enough at first. Nonswimmers are not normally invited to dive in at the deep end!

Think of Christ as a very gracious and understanding person quite near to you. Talk to him now in your mind. Is it a foolish thing to do?

The best people of all the ages have talked to God in their mind. You can only know him personally by personal fellowship, and that means (as it would mean with *any* person) by conversation. Speak to him . . . and listen!

Listen?

Yes! listen. It is not conversation if *you* do all the talking.

Will he answer?

Oh, yes! He'll answer. Do you doubt it? If you are the kind of person who has a flaming temper, the next time you have an outburst stop . . . and listen. Think of him . . . and listen. He will tell you at once that it is wild and vulgar. Or if you are the kind of person who does an underground trade in dirty tales (or snigger at other people's) the next time you tell one or snigger at somebody else's . . . remember him and listen. You will not be in any doubt what he thinks about that.

Nor does he speak only when we do wrong. He speaks in warm approval too. He will restrain you, guide you, encourage you, strengthen you . . . . If you learn to listen, he will not leave you thinking that you are talking to yourself. Out of so simple a beginning as a prayer-conversation with God, maintained each day, he can begin to make himself known to you, and carry you beyond all doubting that he is there and he is kind.

The speed with which he can penetrate your life depends on several things, but chiefly on the regularity and unhurriedness of your daily conversations with him and on your swift obedience to the counsel which he gives. Each part of your personality will help the other. As you think more about him, you cannot help caring more for him and, as you care more, you will want to do the things which please him. Bit by bit, he will work into your life. People who are well advanced in this way of living hardly know where he begins and they leave off. He thinks in their minds and loves in their hearts and wills with their wills. They live lives of constant victory. They are not always in rapture, of course, but they are always in peace.

And they shine with a radiance which comes from their very core—the place which he himself is pleased to fill.

And he, who made the foul-mouthed Peter and the blood-stained Paul radiant, could make you radiant too.

TO SUM UP

The way to certainty in religion requires the same initial venture of trust which swimming requires . . . but no more.

Only as you trust the water can you be sure that it will hold you up.

Only as you trust God can he prove that he is there and enter every part of your nature.

Start trusting him by talking to him . . . and by listening too.

7

FLINGING THE DOOR WIDE OPEN

AND now the time has come for what is primarily an act of will. Any man or woman who has ventured on prayer-conversation with God has come to know that he is there, has felt already within him that the bad is being beaten down and the good built up, and is conscious of deepening desires for the best God has to give.

Yet all this is the fruit of half-casual acquaintanceship. If Christ is to come into our life and "reign without a rival there," we must admit him, eagerly, to every part, with no term put to his stay. The complete transformation he is able to work in a life depends on the completeness of his control and the clear understanding that he is there for good.

God will never bludgeon his way into any man's life. He made us free and he respects the personalities which he has made. All our dealings are with a *courteous* Lord, and he will never intrude when he is unwelcome. While it is clear that the residence of Christ in any man's soul is an act of Christ himself, it is clear also that our unwillingness will keep him out. Those who want the secret of radiant living must first decide therefore whether or not they *want* Christ—really want him, want him in every segment of their nature, and want him "for keeps."

Some things will have to go if he comes in. We cannot continue the practice of things he disapproves. Harbored evil must go. A man who sincerely offers Christ his whole life can still slip—but it is a *slip.* It is not something regularly done and built into the framework of his life. And even if he slips, he never wallows. He finds himself down with an awful shock; apologizes at once to his Master; and, Christ helping him, gets up at once, humbler, wiser, and infinitely more careful to keep in step with his Lord.

The past must be forgiven if Christ is to come in. Everyone has something on his conscience. Ill-used consciences grow coarse, and some people are unaware how much there is to be forgiven until

Christ is actually in residence; but the more he takes control, the more aware of sin we become. And there is so little a human being can do about sin. He can apologize here and sometimes make partial restitution there, but with the central guilt of it he can do nothing. The past is past; it is in the record, and a stain on his life.

People unwilling to face reality often deny the guilt of their guilty conduct, call this talk of "guilt" a foolish "taboo," even succeed sometimes in forgetting it in their conscious mind. But the subconscious mind forgets nothing; and the past lies forgotten but festering, and showing itself sometimes in nervous disorders, in irritability, in constant sarcasm, and in a deep unease, which is hard for the unskilled to diagnose and is completely beyond human cure.

Only God can forgive sins! That is one of the prerogatives of Deity! That was how people first began to suspect that Christ was God on earth. He forgave sins! It is only to God that any man or woman can turn for forgiveness. *And all do need it!*

A skillful psychiatrist can often diagnose a person's trouble as "a conscience distress." But only God can cure it. That is another reason why it is to God that all men and women must turn at the last. To try to dodge the sense of guilt, or to say with affected carelessness that the thing happened "a long time ago," or to dive into atheism as a hide-out from a righteous God, is all fruitless. You are so made that the accusation remains and the condemnation also. They remain within. At a deep level of your life you are *self*-accused and *self*-condemned. A soul stripped, and in the uncreated light of God, could not even pretend.

So why pretend? Go to God for forgiveness now! Out with everything you can remember—and ask him to undertake for the things you cannot remember too. Allow no pride to hinder you at this point. Pride is the first and worst of sins, and on your way to sue for mercy it will tug at your sleeve and seek to persuade you not to go through with it. It will suggest that to sue for mercy is cowardly or undignified or unnecessary. Brush it aside! Go right to God and ask him, for Christ's sake, to forgive you. Do not plead extenuating circumstances or furbish up a few excuses. He knows everything that can be said for you. It is not much, and his mercy does not hinge on that. Your only hope (and it is completely adequate!) is in his own nature revealed most blazingly in the Cross. He loves like that. He is that kind of God. He enjoys forgiving all who are truly sorry. So go to him at once and get it done.

You need no human intermediary to go to God. If you think it would help you, seek out some minister of God and know that your secrets are kept.

But you do not *need* an intermediary. Any man or woman may go direct to God in Christ, and everyone seeking inward peace *must* go to God to get it. Anybody who is not forgiven cannot be a radiant personality. How can he be? Who can be radiant with guilt festering at any level of his mental and emotional life? Radiant personality, as we have seen already, is a by-product. You cannot go for it directly, and the very effort so to do is immature. Saul of Tarsus was not seeking radiance when he gave in to Jesus Christ. He was seeking forgiveness. The radiance came of itself when Christ forgave him and came to live in his committed life.

His unimpeachable word has been given that he will turn no sincere penitent away. Murderers, prostitutes, procurers, warmongers, rapacious business magnates . . . all may come. If they are sincerely sorry, he will not turn them away; and if they are not sorry enough, he will help them even there. You need make no public declaration of this compact with God. Some people are glad of the chance to do so, and some sign a simple declaration of fealty as an aid to themselves. But the essential thing is the secret commerce of a man's soul with his Maker. It is an honest confession of all you remember of sin and a sincere plea for the forgiveness of God. Just that! And for Christ's sake, he will forgive you and (such is his staggering offer!) erase the record as well.

Take his forgiveness! Just take it!—with wonder and delight.

Some silly people go to God for forgiveness and will not believe they have it when they have. They almost make God out to be a liar —as though he does not forgive the penitent though he said he would. They carry their burdens of guilt about still and it prevents any radiance filling their lives. God has forgiven them, but they cannot forgive themselves. In some cases it is a curious twist of unsurrendered pride. Deep in their minds they are saying to themselves: "Fancy *me* ever doing that."

Well, you did it! You were capable of that and guilty of it. So have no pride in yourself, for there is no ground for it, but exult in the fact that the Lord of this universe is a merciful Father who has truly forgiven you and is not pleased that you so cuddle the memory of your misdeeds that you obscure the light he has put in your soul.

If Christ comes in, he must come in as King.

Let there be no doubt in any mind what this great act of submission to Christ involves. It is unconditional surrender. He is now *Lord* over your whole life. As his personality penetrates yours, you will need less and less to pull your will into harmony with his. The two wills will mingle and move as one. But submission to him means that whenever the two wills pull apart (or threaten to) his will must prevail. He is master. He has come into your life not as a servant but as the Lord.

No man knows what the future has in store for him. In giving oneself to Christ one must do so in ignorance of the future. But the principle of his Lordship must be accepted here too, so that it is clearly understood that in any future decisions (the test and possible sacrifice of which we cannot imagine) it is *his* will that shall prevail. We do not belong to ourselves any more. We are committed men and women. If some people still want to boast with Henley that they are "the masters of their fates and the captains of their souls," we are not of their number. Christ is the master of our fate, and into his scarred hands we have been grateful to commit our souls.

If Christ comes in, he must come into every area of life.

Many people through the ages have professed to welcome him as King but have sought to retain their own authority in one area of their life.

Then he is not *King!*

A truly kingly rule is without limit, and it is that kind of rule he asks us willingly to accept. We are not forced to accept it. We are still free with this courteous Lord to say "No."

But we must know what we are doing. It is over *every* area of life that he seeks to rule. Home life, business life, social life, public life, inner life . . . . There is not one inch of territory from which he is willing to be shut out.

When temptation attacks us, it always tries to find something in us to which it can attach itself. It seeks to make a bridgehead in the territory of our soul, and send its sappers over that way. When Christ garrisons a soul to keep it invulnerable from evil, he cannot consent to be excluded from any territory which the enemy could use to get its envoys in.

And because he would be plain with us from the beginning, he wants it to be clear that if he comes in, he must rule in every part.

If Christ comes in, he wants to come in for good.

It is not as a president but as a king that Christ wants to come into our lives. A president serves for a period and goes out of office. A king rules for life.

Our King wants to rule within us for the *whole* of our lives, in time and eternity too.

So let us pause on the verge of this momentous act and entertain no doubt of its magnitude.

He will undertake for our soiled past. He will work with us for the transformation of our present life. He wants our complete and willing committal for ever and ever. He knows we will slip, but that will not be intentional disloyalty. However frail we may be, let it be understood that we do not *intend* at any time to take ourselves back. These are life-vows and meant as such.

Well, are you ready for it? Do you mean it, for every bit of you, and for ever? Does it need to be argued any more?

There is nowhere else you can go with your sin and no one else who can offer in the future such venture and security.

Can you seriously doubt his claim upon you? They called him a Carpenter once, but a third of the world now worships him, and it is a safe guess that more than another third holds him in honest respect. Though God has produced good men in other faiths also, the number and nobility of the Christian saints are without parallel.

Is he not worthy to be your Lord?

Is it indeed not wonderful that he will *take* you?

> *I come, Lord; I believe, Lord; I throw my-self on Thy grace and mercy. . . . Bid me not go away, for I will not go.*

TO SUM UP

We are called now to surrender our lives to Christ.
All of them.
Forever.
If we do that:
He will forgive the past.
Transform the present.
Impart his peace and light.

8

WHAT THIS INVOLVES

The life of God (as shown by Jesus) is a life of loving service and limitless sacrifice. In the bliss of his peace and the rapture of his presence one no more heeds the sacrifice involved than any happy bridegroom would be distressed on his wedding day at being reminded of all the likely girls he had given up in getting married. Filled with joy in securing the one he wanted above all others, he would say: "Look what I've got!" And when the life of God comes into the soul of a man, he does not gloomily foresee the sacrifices it will involve for him, but exults in the deep content in his heart and glows with the sense of having found at last the "something" he had longed for all his days.

Nevertheless, it would be well if we looked at all that is involved lest selfishness intrude again and God be squeezed out of the heart to which he has been invited.

We have already recognized that there can be something deeply selfish even in the engrossing concern for inward peace and outward radiance if those desirable things are considered only as something which "*I* want." An end does not cease to be selfish because it is high and noble. So long as self is central and strident it is still *selfish,* though one is aiming at a virtue or a grace.

This is a moment for complete candor. Even to seek the secret of radiant life as an end in itself and something *you* want is spiritually impossible. It is self-defeating. God made this peace and radiance (as we have already said) a by-product. Open your nature to the life of God; welcome the Eternal to your narrow heart, and peace and radiance will be yours . . . but only so long as his life is allowed the ruling place in yours and streams through you to other people. Paradoxical as it may sound, God can only stay in you when he passes through you. To covet God just for what *you* are going to get out of him is blasphemous and contradictory in its very essence.

When the life of God comes into a human soul, it is still the life of God. It cannot be other than it is. It is of the nature of God to love without limit and reach out in blessing to all. He comes gladly into any willing heart *that he may pass through it in blessing to others.* But the love of God is not dammed. Where it cannot pass through, it cannot fully inflow. Where Christians do not give themselves to service, aridity returns. It must do so. The divine law is: "Give, *and it shall be given unto you* . . . ." Don't give and it can't be given. Inward peace and true radiance don't belong to selfishness by the very principles on which the universe is built—principles which are simply an expression of the nature of God.

All this is made clear in the life of Christ. His whole life was obedience. He came to do the will of him who sent him. From "the poor manger to the bitter cross" he was saying "Yes" to his Father's will. His whole life was spent in the service of others . . . and it is to that life that we have now surrendered ourselves and it is that life which seeks to *manifest* itself through us.

People have heard (quite truly) that a new spiritual experience often cures physical ills. Doctors have known for years past that psychosomatic sickness often yields to religious insight and sick people sometimes come to God *just to be made well.* For nothing else: to go on living the same selfish lives they were living before. Is it any wonder that nothing happens . . . or if it happens, that it does not last?

People have sought peace and radiance on the same terms: "Give me *that* . . . and let me go on being the same self-engrossed person that I was before." The kindest thing that one can say about such pleadings is that "they know not what they ask." They would make God the accomplice of their chronic selfishness and "use" the Deity for their own ends.

The most radiant Christians I have known were never self-consciously so. God indwelt them and they were lost in service for others. Most of them had little of this world's goods. Some were giving their leisure in the slums, some were serving on the mission field, some fighting social evils, and some (in the eventide of their days) giving all their time to intercession.

One proof of the divine indwelling was their lack of concern about themselves. All their life was prayer and love. It could be said of them as it was said of Samuel Barnett of Toynbee Hall: "He forgot himself to the extent of forgetting that he had forgotten."

To that, then, we are now gladly and humbly committed. God may do with us what he wills. We recognize again that while it was natural for us to want peace and radiance, we might as well forget about them. They will come in on the side while we are engrossed in doing God's will. In our gazing into the mirror of Christ (as we must do later) to discover the people we are, and in our study of the techniques by which we may open ourselves to the life of God, this thought will be in our minds all the time: that it is the life *of God* which is coming into us and it only comes fully *in* as it is allowed to go freely *through*. It cannot be the life of God *in* us if it does not become the service of men *by* us.

> Freely to all ourselves we give,
> Constrained by Jesus' love to live,
> The servants of mankind.

TO SUM UP

Engrossing concern for inward peace and outward radiance can be selfish.

Both are by-products of God in the soul, but God in the soul involves service and sacrifice.

Asking for peace and radiance as additions to a selfish life is asking the impossible.

God only stays in us as he passes through us.

9

WHY ARE SOME CHRISTIANS *NOT* RADIANT?

A CHURCH official paused one Saturday evening on the fringe of a Salvation Army meeting in the open air. He was one of those grim-looking men who sometimes hold office in the church. (Nobody doubts their integrity, but nobody wants to be like them.) All the lines of his face seemed to run down at acute angles, as though he lived all the while with an unpleasant odor under his nose, and he looked the very opposite of all that we mean by radiance.

One of the Salvation Army lassies, hovering on the outskirts of the crowd, asked him if he was saved. Embarrassed by the question, he replied tartly: "I hope I am."

According to the report, the girl who asked the question called out to the leader of the meeting: "He says that he *hopes* he is saved. *What a face for a child of God!"*

Now that poses a question we can no longer avoid. Why is it that many people in the church, whose character and Christian standing we cannot possibly doubt, lack the radiance which we say is the inevitable consequence of Christ living within? They are emphatically not hypocrites; they are good men and women. But they are not radiant or even clearly and quietly serene, and they do not put a longing in other people to share the life they claim to possess.

It is an undoubted fact that many people outside the churches think that if they become Christians they will become miserable. They think that life in Christ is less and less rather than more and more. They think that it is giving up most of the things which make glad the heart of man. At the mere thought of entering this way of life, something chill strikes at the heart of them and they race away like animals almost trapped. And they are sincere!

How came this wide illusion to infect the thought of honest people? Are we Christians not compelled to admit that—somehow or other—we have given the impression that Christianity is anything but abundant and radiant life? Does not our general demeanor often suggest that religion is a heavy load which we are carrying rather than something which carries us? And is there much hope that the Church will impress the world unless its members recover this conquering life—and the radiance which is its outward expression?

I met a depressed minister the other day. He had been suffering from gastric ulcers and his local doctor had sent him to a specialist.

"He examined me with great care," he explained, "and then he told me that there was no reason really why I should have the ulcers. 'I suspect that you have a worrying nature,' he said. 'Trifles fret and annoy you. If only you could take things more calmly, trust more, and keep quiet inside you . . .' "

And here the poor minister almost broke down. "I was never so humiliated in my life," he said. "A doctor of medicine talking to *me* like that!"

Then he added: "And the bitterest part of it all is this—that I know what he said was true."

We may as well face it. Many of us are not good samples of the faith we profess. We affirm our fixed belief that we have a divine Father who has numbered the hairs of our head and is watching over us all the time for good . . . and yet we worry! We are sub-Christian. John Wesley—that robust Christian—said: "I could no more worry than I could curse or swear."

We claim as Christians that the center of our life has been shifted from ourselves to Christ . . . yet some of us are chronically selfish still. We say that the first of all the graces is humility . . . but we are proud. We talk of "a peace that passes all understanding" . . . yet we are restless within, and our inner restlessness betrays itself in a lack of repose. We claim to be "children of the heavenly King" . . . but we still feel inferior. We say that from the heart of the Christian perfect love has cast out fear . . . but we are as fearful as the next man. Daily we pray that we may be forgiven our trespasses, *"as we forgive those who trespass against us"* . . . yet we harbor resentments and are not strangers to bitterness. "There is no joy like the joy of a Christian," we have said . . . but we are moody. We complain over trifles, are sometimes guilty of meanness, and time and time again are negative in our thought.

It is true that we do not swear, steal, get drunk, or philander with the other sex, but neither do thousands of people who make no claim to be Christians at all. People who watch us closely are not commonly struck by our radiance and forced to believe that we have some deep and secret joy. With our worries, inferiorities, complaints, and moodiness we seem just like the worldly . . . except that when they go to the movies on Sunday evening we go to church. But how much does it do for us?

If Christians are people in whom Christ lives, how does it happen that many of us give so little evidence that he is inside us? If he has the secret of radiant personality, how came we to miss it? Can a man be a Christian and be a stranger to this inner light?

We must be frank. The term "Christian," as it is commonly used, is a vague term. Many people are regarded as Christians because they were born into a nominally Christian country, though they never go to a church and know next to nothing of the faith. Others regard themselves as Christians because they were baptized, though—like vaccination sometimes—it did not "take." Some base their claim to the title on an occasional visit to church (on Easter Sunday perhaps) and the fact that they have kept out of the hands of the police. Still others have made an honest dedication of their life to God but have experienced no conscious inflow of divine power, and life is toiling self-effort for them—as much after their dedication as it was before.

Some think that it all depends on knowledge—but that oversimplifies it! Is an eminent and scholarly theologian who cannot keep his temper more a Christian than a charwoman who can—even though (alas!) she cannot repeat the Apostles' Creed? Is the famous and popular preacher who is proud more a Christian than the church caretaker who is humble?

I would be loath to deny the name of "Christian" to any man who earnestly claimed it for himself. Only God knows the depth of sincerity within us and the divine help we have resisted and received.

But this we *can* know—each one of us for himself. With the New Testament open before us, and the picture of Christ plainly in view, and our consciences allowed to give an honest testimony in our souls . . . we have not been the men and women we might have been; we have lived on a lower level than the New Testament teaches us as normal; we have not "sold" our way of life in the world by the obvious poise and gladness which it gave to us; we have not made the worldly think that we have something they dare not miss.

All the saints of God have joy. It is one of their marks. St. Francis of Assisi was God's minstrel. St. Teresa frowned on frowns! Reformer though she was, she would take the castanets and dance like a girl in the hour of recreation with her delighted nuns. Plymouth brethren are supposed (by those who do not know them) always to be solemn, but Edmund Gosse, who grew up in such a home (and broke from it), gladly conceded that there was nothing gloomy about his home; it was a place of wholesome jokes, innocent laughter, "always cheerful and often gay."

Who could help being radiant with God living in them?—who could mope and fret who *honestly believed* that Infinite Wisdom and Infinite Love were attending to all things?

But why are some Christians so grim?

The best of these people have surrendered their *wills* to Christ, but have never given him full control of their minds. They are, in a sense, dedicated men and women; but Christ has never been allowed to reshape their thinking. And thought is life! The Bible says: "As a man thinks in his heart, so is he." These joyless powerless Christians acknowledge Christ as Lord and may do nothing deliberately to displease him, but their thinking continues on the old low level; and so fear and inferiority, restlessness and resentment, pride and complaining, can still have a major place in their life. So far as the *mind* is concerned, Christ is not in them. Sometimes knowingly—but usually *un*knowingly—they have kept Christ out of their thinking and they are almost the same defeated people that they were before they took him as Lord.

This is what Paul, who knew more than most men what an utter transformation Christ's indwelling could make, would say to them:

> Be ye transformed by the renewing of your mind.
> Have this mind in you, which was also in Christ Jesus. (A.S.V.)
> Be renewed in the spirit of your mind.

If Christ is not in our *minds* (in the warp and woof of our thinking), he is not in us, and "a Christ not in us is a Christ not ours."

TO SUM UP

Some Christians are rather grim people.

Many Christians lack poise and radiance.

How can this be if peace and happiness are the inevitable consequences of having Christ within?

The answer is this: many of them have yielded their *wills* to him but never fully their *minds*.

The New Testament says plainly that it is *by the renewing of our minds* that we are *transformed*.

10

DO WE LACK THE *MIND* OF CHRIST?

Not everybody is willing to admit that his mind needs to be transformed. "What is wrong with *my* mind?" some ask. "I am a perfectly normal person."

There is an enormous difference between what the world accepts as normal and what the New Testament teaches as normal. In the world it is accepted as normal for a man to quarrel on occasion, to look after "number one" most of the time, to harbor resentment if he has been unfairly treated (or thinks he has!) and to have his periods of ill temper. None of these things belongs to the Christian life as the New Testament pictures it. By the power of the indwelling Christ, life can be lived above all these wrong humors and lived on that level *without strain*. Such a conquering life is not the fruit of toiling self-effort but of an "alert passivity" which eagerly receives the life of God into the soul and lives by his power. There are not many people faced with that contrast and convinced of the possibility of this change who would deny that their lives need to be transformed.

We can be honestly and deeply ignorant of ourselves. Yet no real progress is possible without self-knowledge.

Socrates—the wisest man of his age—greeted all his new pupils with the words: "Know thyself."

So deep is our self-ignorance that it cannot be doubted that there are millions of people in the world guilty of faults which stick out a yard in the gaze of all their acquaintances *but of which they are completely unaware themselves*. They see other people's faults clearly. *But not their own!*

Perhaps it is not altogether surprising. They are on the dark side of them. They are like motorists slashing along at speed through the wet night, complaining with scorn of the blazing headlights of every car coming the opposite way and blissfully unaware of the blinding glare of their own lights in the other man's eyes.

How can we see ourselves? No man will really put himself in Christ's transforming school until self-knowledge and the failure to put himself right make him sick in self-despair.

Fulton Oursler once told the story of a man—his name was Frank Dudley—whose life was changed by three brief telephone calls. At least, the change *began* that way. That was the means by which he came to self-knowledge.

Born in poverty, he had managed by sheer grit to put himself and his younger brother through college. With the passing years he became quite a business magnate, while his brother secured a post as a lecturer in history.

Frank Dudley always felt paternal toward his brother Eddie. He was older. He had found the money for his brother's college course. He loved to keep a fatherly eye on him and watch his academic progress. When Eddie married, Frank did not feel very closely drawn to Agnes (his sister-in-law), but he did his best to be good friends with her because he wanted no barrier from Eddie. In course of time Eddie got a college appointment in another town, and he and Agnes moved away.

It was on a visit to this other town that Frank Dudley had those three telephone calls. He rang up his brother's home. Agnes answered, and he asked her if she and Eddie would come to dinner with him that night.

"No, thanks!" she said. "Eddie has a business appointment, and I'm busy too. Eddie will ring you."

Disappointed at that, he rang up an old college friend and asked him to join him at dinner. His friend said: "Dinner? We're going to a party at Eddie and Agnes'. We'll see you there!"

Staggered at that scrap of news, Dudley had hardly replaced the receiver when the phone rang. It was his brother. Eddie said: "Sorry I'm tied up tonight, Frank. How about lunch tomorrow?"

Frank Dudley mumbled his assent and hung up.

So they were having a party and they did not want him there! They had lied to him. Next morning, when his brother had gone to his lecturing, Frank called on his sister-in-law and had it out.

She was very open. "Eddie wanted you at the party," she said, "but I didn't! You would have spoiled everything."

"How can you say such a thing?" he asked.

Then she let him have it.

"We came to this town," she said, "to get away from you. You dominate everything. You are the big successful businessman! The conversation *must* center in you, wherever you are. If Eddie tells a story and you are there, you tell a better one. If he expresses an opinion, you contradict it and make him look foolish. . . . There is a chance of Eddie's getting a rather important post, and the people who were coming to our party might influence the decision. I wanted Eddie to appear at his best last evening, and that meant I had to keep you away. . . ."

When Dudley protested that he was not *that* kind of person, his sister-in-law said with a touch of scorn: "Aren't you? You ought to get wise to yourself."

You ought to get wise to yourself.

That is advice we could all take. In fact, Frank Dudley did get wise to himself . . . and discovered that his sister-in-law was right. He watched himself and found that he did not really listen to other people's stories: he was thinking of a better one to steal the laugh. He found that he spiced his conversation with gossip, uttered little depreciations even of his friends, felt secretly elated over other people's misfortunes, and actually grieved at their big successes.[1]

He had lived to middle age before he "got wise to himself." Many people die still not wise to themselves. Yet no real spiritual progress is possible without that wisdom.

There is one sovereign way to this wisdom: probably only one. *We must see ourselves in Christ.*

Nobody really sees himself until he sees himself in Christ. Christ is a mirror. He reflects a perfect likeness of the image which falls on him. A man can look at himself in the mirror which is Christ and say with truth: "That is the man I am." To a sensitized conscience, the revelation can be appalling, and we might be grateful to God that he saves us from seeing all the truth at a glance. But we must be more grateful that he allows us to see the truth about ourselves at all—and see it where alone it can be seen: *in him.*

[1] From *The Hardest Lesson* by Fulton Oursler. Copyright 1952 by The Hearst Corporation, reprinted by permission of Doubleday & Co., Inc.

Sometimes our enemies tell us what they think about us, but they usually exaggerate our faults and speak in anger, so we toss their words aside. They never pierce the armor of our self-esteem.

Quite often those most near and dear to us are blinded by their love to our failings, or if they see them, they bear with us for their love's sake.

What we need if we are to advance from self-knowledge to victory is Someone who sees into the very heart of us, loves us deeply . . . but will never let us off.

We have all three in Christ. He sees into the heart of us, loves us deeply, but will never let us off.

During the First World War a soldier on the battlefields of France picked up in the ruins of a church a rather nice frame which had once contained a picture of Christ. Embossed on the bottom of the frame were the words *"Ecce Homo"* ("Behold the man!"). He sent it home as a souvenir; and someone at home straightened the frame, put a mirror in it, and hung it in the parlor.

A visitor called at the house soon after. Asked to wait a few minutes in the parlor, he was glancing round the little room when he read the startling words, "Behold the man!"—and saw *himself*.

That is where we *can* see ourselves. In Christ!

TO SUM UP

Many people deny that their minds need to be transformed.

But few men know themselves.

Most of us are guilty of faults all our friends notice but of which we are totally unaware.

The one sure way to self-knowledge is *to see ourselves in Christ.*

PART TWO

THE TRUTH

The Person I Am

11

AM I WRAPPED UP IN MYSELF?

Our aim, then, is to see ourselves *in* Christ; to compare and contrast the persons we are to the Person he is; to make a mirror, as it were, of the divine life revealed to us in the four Gospels, and come to know the persons we are as we gaze on the picture he drew.

Necessarily this will involve much work on the Bible and especially on the records we have of the life of Christ himself. We shall treat the book as a manual and allow no proper reverence for it to hinder its workmanlike use. We can thumb it, mark it, wear it out, and buy another. If we are to see ourselves in Christ, we must know his life with an intimacy we may never have thought necessary till now. There is no other way. Only as we gaze steadily into the mirror can we see ourselves as we are.

Let us look, then, at ourselves *in Christ.*

The first thing which strikes any man or woman who seriously conducts this kind of self-examination is how preoccupied we are with ourselves—and not only, or chiefly, when we are engaged in self-examination, but at all times. In the natural man everything seems to have an immediate self-reference. The instant reaction of normal nature to any event or piece of news or future possibility is "How will this affect *me?*" The average man is far more distressed by a trifling mishap to himself than by a major calamity in someone else's life. Our self-preoccupation is so natural and common that it has long been accepted as normal; it is only when we *make* ourselves face it that the enormity and distortion of our selfishness really appears.

I was talking to the football coach of one of our public schools in the summer of 1939, and he said most earnestly that he hoped there would not be a war. Then he added: "You see, I think I shall have the finest football team next season the school has ever known!"

Traveling by train from Hull to London recently, I heard a lady falteringly tell another lady in the next seat that she was in great grief; she had recently lost her husband. The lady to whom she gave her confidence expressed her instant sympathy. "I can feel for you," she said, "I recently lost my dog!"

The commoner forms of selfishness have long since ceased to excite comment: diving for the best chair, breaking in line when possible, monopolizing the conversation, always getting the best of the bargain, boring other people with talk of your wonderful children or grandchildren, and barely concealing your disinterest when they talk of theirs. How chronic it is—this absorbing self-centeredness! Many people have come to accept it as ineradicable in human nature, and any hope of freedom from it they regard as fanciful and "perfectionist."

It belongs to the essential sanity of Christianity that it recognizes the legitimacy of *self-love*. Jesus quoted with approval the Hebrew law: "Thou shalt love thy neighbor *as thyself*." One great world faith denies the value of individuals or any separate eternity for them; Christianity affirms both.

There is a form of mental illness known to all psychiatrists which is really self-hate. Millions of people secretly despise themselves; and some, as we know, hate life so much that they commit suicide. Christianity never countenances self-hate and self-torture. Though this has appeared occasionally in the long history of the Church, it was an unconscious caricature of the faith. Christianity declares the legitimacy of self-love—just so long as it is not love *only* for the self, and not sought singly, and never divorced from the equal love of others.

It is from *self-centeredness* that Christ would deliver us. It is that arrogant, thrustful, debased, and dominating self that he would crucify, and having crucified, replace with his own gloriously unselfish life.

Aware as all honest men and women are of the deep selfishness of their nature, and conscious as most of us are also of our inability to save ourselves, let us turn (and with this in mind) to the study of the life of Jesus Christ.

Charles Wesley said once to his Lord: "All thy life was prayer and love," and a reverent study of the Gospels confirms that summary. His first thought was not of himself, but to do his Father's will, and his Father's will was one of costly service to the sons of men.

All the record is one of devotion to the needs of others. Peter summarized his life by saying: "He went about doing good." (R.S.V.) He fed the hungry, cheered the sad, healed the sick, and preached good tidings to the poor. Possessed of powers far above the normal, he did not use them for his own comfort, aggrandizement, or gain. In him there moved on the surface of this planet for the only time in history (so students of the New Testament believe) a completely *un*-self-centered person. Even his fierce denunciation of the religious leaders of his day cannot be interpreted (in the steady light of his life taken as a whole) as personal resentment of their opposition to him, but as the desperate warnings of love uttered to those treading the way to hell. Go over the record set down nearly two thousand years ago by the four evangelists and you will find nothing on which you can convict this man of selfishness. All his life was prayer and love.

Nowhere is this more evident than in his last hours. His execution was the greatest crime in history. Nothing so concisely convicts the human race of wickedness than that it could do nothing with this perfect Life but murder it. The timing of his last day is difficult to work out with exactness, but it appears that in the brief space of six hours he was "tried" five times by four different tribunals. He was accused by witnesses who contradicted themselves, condemned on a deliberate misinterpretation of his words, and sentenced by a judge convinced of his innocence.

Yet in the face of this accumulated wickedness, he showed no self-pity and (after the agony of Gethsemane) no deep self-concern. Study in particular his whole demeanor from the kiss of Judas till he cried with a loud voice and gave up his spirit. His thought is all the time of others. His strange silence in the judgment hall is explained in part by the high priest's question about his disciples. He was determined to say nothing about them. In the very moment of his arrest in the garden, he hastened to identify himself to the officers in charge of the soldiers in order that his friends could get quickly away. "I am the man you want," he repeated, almost pushing himself at them: "Let these others go."

In the high priest's palace, as the malevolent questioning began, his thought was still so little of himself that he could think on Peter—thrice-denying, brokenhearted Peter—and save him with a look. On the road to the cross itself, his thought is still so little of himself that he pauses to speak to the weeping women: "Weep not for me, but weep for yourselves, and for your children." When the nails are pointed to his palms and his feet and the swinging hammer drives the iron through his yielding flesh, all his pain leaps out in prayer for those who did it: "Father, forgive them: for they know not what they do." When the cross is reared between earth and heaven, and drops with a thud into the waiting hole, and he sags stark naked on the wood in the gaze of all the men and women, it is still of others he is thinking. The blood smears his body and drips to the earth, but he has things to do before he can die. He has comfort for the penitent thief. He makes provision for his desolate mother. Only when every need has been met, and the darkness endured, and the loving heart of God revealed to men forever, does he turn to his Father and seek leave to die. And at a glance from his Father found gloriously near again after that lost sense of his presence, he cries with a loud voice: "It is finished!" And finished it was! Sin beaten. Love victorious. Death defeated. Heaven opened. God revealed.

Let any man or woman look into the mirror of that amazing love and unselfishness and then contrast it with himself. *His* mind so centered in the will of God and the service of others. *Our* mind so preoccupied with me . . . me . . . me.

Have this mind in you, which was also in Christ Jesus. (*A.S.V.*)

TO SUM UP

The normal man is tightly wrapped up in himself.

Selfishness is indeed so widespread and chronic that people barely comment on it or expect a cure.

There is a legitimate self-love but no legitimate self-centeredness.

Christ was utterly un-self-centered.

All his life was prayer and love.

12

DO I THINK MYSELF SOMEBODY?

SELF-CENTEREDNESS is not the only discovery which some of us make as we gaze on ourselves in the mirror of Christ. Many of us discover also that we have an enormous *self-esteem*. It is not only that we are constantly thinking of ourselves; some of us think *so much* of ourselves. It is not merely self-engrossment; it is self-glorification too. The man in the street calls it "pride" and "vanity," and all the old experts in the art of living classified pride as "the deadliest of the deadly sins."

Now that surprises some people. "What is so deadly about pride?" they ask. "It may be silly. It is usually mistaken. But what harm does it do if a fellow thinks a lot of himself? It can't possibly be as bad as lust, or cruelty, or greed."

It is worse! When one really understands what pride is, it is seen as the primal sin and the foulest of them all. It can even make virtue vicious and the other vices more vicious than they were. It is shallow thinking which dismisses pride as something venial and half-harmless, a thing to wave off with a tolerant smile.

Pride puts oneself in the center of life—which is God's place. Pride not only puts oneself in the center of life but exults in having it there. Idolatry, at any time, is an offense to the living God, but no idolatry is so vulgar and offensive as the idolatry of self. The poor benighted heathen worshiping the sun is not so low and vain and foolish as a man worshiping himself.

Pride not only denies that God is the center and soul of the universe but relegates every other mortal to a minor role in it. The really proud man never sees other persons as persons but as small-part actors in a play in which he is the great figure. If circumstances blur—even momentarily—his supreme greatness, how annoyed he can be! The valet of the last German kaiser said: "I cannot deny that my master was vain. He had to be (as All Highest) the central figure in everything. If he went to a christening, he wanted to be the baby. If he went to a wedding, he wanted to be the bride. If he went to a funeral, he wanted to be the corpse." Before we laugh at the kaiser, let us look still more intently in the Mirror to see how much pride lurks in our own vain hearts. A man told me once that he had been in a hospital and had a nurse so conceited that whenever she took the pulse of one of the men she always knocked off five points to allow for the impact of her personality upon the patient!

Pride builds barriers all through human society. It is pride which built the class barriers and produced the centuries of hate and bitterness begotten by them. It is pride which built the barriers between the nations and produced a hundred wars to prove that a German was better than a Frenchman, or a Russian than a Pole! It is pride which builds the barriers between the races and leaves a white man feeling superior to a yellow man, and a brown man to a black. As I write, my eye falls on the newspaper and I learn of the protests made before the Delhi Rotary Club by some African students who claimed that during three years in India they had suffered "immense psychological torture" from racial discrimination and color prejudice, which seemed to them as bad in India as anywhere in the world.

It is pride which builds the barriers between man and God. Man claims to be the measure of all things, to be able to run his "own" world (How did it become "his"?), to solve his own problems, and to secure his own salvation. Pride tampers with the psalms (as A. C. Craig has shown) and says:

> O Man, how excellent is thy name in all the earth! Who has set thy glory above the heavens. When I consider thine inventions, the work of thy fingers, the airplanes and atomic bombs which thou hast made, what is God that I should be mindful of *him,* or the Son of God should I reverence *him?"*

Did you think pride was a half-harmless venial sin? It is the devil's finished handiwork. It made him what he is. It would make this fair earth as "black as the pit from pole to pole."

I said just now that pride makes virtue vicious and the other vices more vicious than they were.

To its other evil distinctiveness pride adds this—that it is the only vice which snatches opportunity from our virtues. The other vices grow in the soil of vice: theft out of covetousness, fornication out of lewd desire, murder out of burning hate . . . . But pride is more subtle. It ensnares people nigh to being saints. When a man (like the Pharisee) has made himself a walking embodiment of the Ten Commandments and a paragon of all the virtues, pride squeezes a little of her juice into his soul and he begins to strut and think, "What a good boy am I! I am vastly superior to these publicans." He does not trace his success to the grace of God, which alone made it possible. He thinks *he* did it . . . and within hailing distance of the serene summit of sanctity, he toboggans to the bottom again. Is anything more nauseating than *self-righteousness?* And what is self-righteousness but pride in one's own goodness?

Nor does the subtlety of pride end even there. It can even trap us by making us feel superior to those it has already trapped. An old lady listened approvingly to a sermon on the Pharisee and publican and went home glowing with inward virtue and saying to her friends: "Well, thank God, *I'm not like them Pharisees!*"

How does pride add to the viciousness of the other vices?

Calculated meanness and deliberate seduction are both, in their different ways, so disgusting to any decent man that he might suppose that nothing in that classification could be worse. Yet it can! Let pride be added to either condition and the beastly becomes beastlier still. Ever heard a mean man boasting of his meanness?—what skill he has developed in stepping out at the right moment and leaving his pals to pay? Ever heard a practiced seducer boasting of the number of trusting foolish girls he has started on the road to hell? Here is something so evil that a decent man can barely prevent himself from vomiting—and it is the admixture of pride in the evil thing which adds the last sickening savor to the whole.

No wonder William Law said: "Pride must die in you, or nothing in heaven can live in you . . . . Look not at pride only as an unbecoming temper, nor at humility only as a decent virtue. . . . One is all hell and the other all heaven!"

And—as we gaze into the mirror of Christ—we see pride in ourselves. It takes varied forms, and some may *not* see it. But most of us do. We remember insults long after we have forgotten sorrows. We bridle if someone treats us with contempt and recall the experience with inward anger twenty years after. We are touchy about our birth, our status, our ability . . . . All these are marks of pride.

Let us look into the life of the Lord Jesus Christ and—with this first of the vices chiefly in mind—see ourselves clearly in him.

Many of us are proud of our *status*. But he was God and laid his glory by. He emptied himself of all but love. He did not abhor the Virgin's womb.

Many of us are proud of our *birth*. But his supposed parents were nor married when he was born, and though we do not talk of it, who can doubt that the tongues of the scandalmongers wagged when Mary went home with her baby in her arms? They have been wagging ever since.

Many of us are proud of our *family*. He grew up in the poor home of a peasant.

Some of us are proud of our *profession*. He was a carpenter.

Some people are proud of their *home*. He had not where to lay his head.

Some folk boast of their *wealth*. He was grateful to be given a meal.

Many people are proud of their *distinguished friends*. His friends were fisherfolk.

Some take pride in their *learning*. He never went to college at all.

Some people move in *high social circles*. He went to the homes of publicans and sinners.

Many men are proud of their *ability*. He said: "I can do nothing of myself."

Some people talk much of *getting their own way*. He said: "I seek not my own will." (R.S.V.)

Some people boast of their *position*. He said: "I am among you as one that serveth."

Many people are proud of their *reputation*. He made himself of no reputation.

Well . . . how do you appear even to yourself in the mirror of that amazing humility? Does it not make your mind reel to think of God in the guise of a servant?

Where does *your* pride lie? in your birth? work? education? ability? friends? reputation? . . . And does he not shame you as you see yourself in him?

He had no pride. People who play with the meaning of words and plead that there is such a thing as "good pride" hate to think of Jesus without pride. They are muddled in their thinking. They are admiring the dignity of meekness, his utter integrity, and his quiet mastery of life. They use the wrong word. Perhaps it will help them to see him again on the last night of his incarnate life.

It was the feast of the Passover. Jesus had secretly borrowed a room to keep the feast, and he and his twelve friends, tired with their long day, made their way to the upper room. All was ready: not only the meal, but the water jugs and basins and towels which served in the East for our modern bathroom. One needs a wash before a meal. The law of Moses required it, but so did a sense of comfort and a concern for hygiene. And not for the face and hands only! Tramping about dirty, hot, and dusty roads all day in sandals left one in special need of clean feet.

But there was no servant present. Normally this was the work of a menial. Maybe Jesus and his friends could not afford a hired servant. Or the secrecy they had to observe made it unwise to engage one. Or the servants themselves were observing the Passover elsewhere. Anyhow, it didn't matter. Any one of the disciples would be eager to do this service for the rest.

Then Jesus noticed it. They were *not* eager—not any one of them—to render this service to the rest. Nobody went for the basin. They looked at one another with that "Who do you think I am?" look in their eye. Peter, no doubt, felt, "It can't be me. After the Master, I'm number one in this outfit." James and John were just as sure that it wasn't their job. They reckoned themselves in the "inner circle" among the apostles. Hadn't they witnessed the Transfiguration and been selected for other favors? Philip and Simon the Zealot felt just as tired as anybody else. Not even the self-effacing Andrew covered up for the rest.

So it was, then, that Jesus himself took off his outer robe, picked up the towel, took the basin, and knelt down and washed his disciples' dirty feet. Each in turn, and not excepting the traitor, *he washed their feet.*

See him there! This is either sublime or blasphemous. Celsus (in the second century) found it blasphemous. It was one of the things he had against the Christians that they were so low-minded that they pictured God, not only crucified, but washing people's muddy feet. He held such an idea to be utterly profane, and until you come almost where Celsus was, you will not see it for the sublime incredibility that it is.

We sometimes call this deed of our Lord in the upper room an "acted parable," but whatever you think of it, do not think of it as play-acting: something just put on to point a moral. It arose in the context of events. It was his answer to their pride. In one stroke he swept from the pedestal of man's esteem the idea that the great man is one who lords it over others, gives orders, remains "uncontaminated" by simple service, and gets higher and higher, the farther and farther he gets from hard work. "That is not the ideal," he says. "The greatest man must become like a junior and the leader must be a servant. I am among you as one who serves."

That is what he said and that is how he lived.

In the mirror of his lowly mind we see our own vile vanity. One thing remains!—that we go to Calvary and pour contempt on all our pride.

Have this mind in you, which was also in Christ Jesus. (*A.S.V.*)

TO SUM UP

Not only are we full of self-concern.
Many of us are full of self-esteem,
vain,
inflated,
proud.
Pride is the deadliest disease of the soul.
It builds barriers, creates wars, and aims to elbow God out of his own world.
It can poison the virtues and make the other vices still more vicious.
From his conception to his crucifixion, Christ's life was all humility.
He actually washed his disciples' feet.

13

WHAT IS THIS INNER UNREST?

DISINCLINED though many people are to admit it, there is a sense of unease and dissatisfaction in the heart of any man or woman until he is at ease with God. Right at the core of our being there is a hunger for something hard to define and almost embarrassing to confess, but which still remains when this world has given us its finest things and every tangible fear has been driven away. Some people say that it is the longing in us for the eternal—a kind of homesickness of the soul.

William Watson knew it. He said:

In this house with starry dome
Shall I never feel at home? [1]

Never! The fact must be faced that, though man seems to belong to the earth, there is a hunger in him which earth cannot satisfy. It seems to satisfy the birds and the beasts. They eat their fill and are content. But man does not live by bread alone. He has immortal longings in him.

This deep truth is concealed from many people because they have material wants unsatisfied and they spend their days struggling for these material things, convinced that they would be blissfully happy could they only possess them. And because many of them die not having achieved the particular *thing* they were after, they die in ignorance of the fact that it could not have satisfied them even if it had been theirs. Or not for long! A month or six months later, a year, or a year or two, and that ache would have reasserted itself in the soul. Any wife and mother knows how hard it is to satisfy husband or son when he comes to the table saying peevishly, "I feel I want something . . . *but I don't know what it is that I want* . . . ." The skillful housewife can usually fix some dish on which that vague appetite can focus, but

[1] *The Poems of Sir William Watson 1878-1935.* Used by permission of the publishers, George G. Harrap and Company.

nothing made or grown on this planet can satisfy the deepest longings of our soul. Augustine's famous words echo in our minds again: "Thou hast made us for Thyself, and our heart is restless till it finds rest in Thee."

People not in good physical health, and longing with all their nature to be really well, would take a lot of convincing that perfect health would not be perfect bliss. But it wouldn't! The finest specimen of physical fitness I ever met was a doctor who came to me as a patient with a very sick soul. He would not have remained physically fit much longer had his spiritual condition not been drastically dealt with.

Millions of people spend their lives longing for more money, dreaming of a legacy or a lucky investment or a big win on the race track. Some of them are almost sick with desire. I have known a few rich men but they were not the happiest men of my acquaintance, and such happiness as they had did not derive chiefly from their wealth.

Every normal man and woman has many things infinitely more precious than a fortune—e.g., their sight, a clear mind, friendship, a sense of wonder—but they eat their hearts out for money they would part with instantly if it were necessary to buy back something they already possess. How much money would you give for your sight?

And not all the money in the world could satisfy that deep hunger of the soul. Jay Gould, with fifty million dollars, said: "I suppose I am the most miserable devil alive."

Human love is the longing with millions of others—as natural, I suppose, as the longing for fitness and wealth. Earth has nothing better to give than this. Indeed, at its purest it partakes of heaven as well as of earth, yet by itself alone it is still incapable of quenching that secret thirst of the soul. I remember the charming young woman who told me that she had not a care in the world: happily married, children growing up nicely, plenty of friends . . . but (she said it in some confusion):

> I'm half ashamed to admit that I'm still wanting something I can't clearly define. Sometimes I think it is just interior peace, and sometimes I think it is a bigger purpose in life, and sometimes I fancy I need to see more plainly into the meaning of things . . . and sometimes I wonder if it is *just God.*

George Herbert said in a quaint poem that God made man with "a glass of blessings standing by," and poured the blessings on his creature till only one was left in the glass. It was the blessing of inward rest. Then God stayed his hand. Fearful that having all things man would never seek his God, the great Artificer said:

> Let him be rich and weary, that at least,
> If goodness lead him not, yet weariness
>   May toss him to My breast.

So we were made—with an ache within which only God can assuage, a thirst in the soul which no water of earth can satisfy, a hunger unmet except by the manna which falls from above.

It is when we look into the mirror of Christ and see him poised in perfect peace upon his Father that we sense more sharply the fret and dissatisfaction in our own souls.

Study the Gospels with the closest care, and in every situation (the Garden of Gethsemane apart) Jesus is master of it. There is no sense of rush or impatience or breathlessness about him. He goes calmly and serenely on his way.

Now this would be remarkable in any man, but how much more remarkable it is when we remember the enormous pressure under which he worked and his awareness that nothing would satisfy his enemies but his utter defeat and death? Yet—so sure is he of his divine mission, so certain that he is in his Father's will, so confident that nothing can ultimately defeat the strategy of God—he goes quietly forward without anxiety, instability, or haste.

All the time *he has time*—time for a thoughtful inquirer like Nicodemus and time for the loose woman at the well, time to go to a wedding and time to watch children at their play. He remains unruffled by interruption, opposition, or even by wickedness directed against himself. He lays himself on the two pieces of wood and continues to talk to his Father with complete certainty that this culminating wickedness will finally bear his message and not theirs—as indeed it does. The cross, which they meant to be an ineradicable stigma, blazes with the glory of his unspeakable love. The sign they judged to be so hideous that even his followers would hush it up tops our tallest steeples and serves as our symbol of victory.

Here are two simple ways of testing his unearthly peace. Let us follow him, in imagination, for a couple of typical days in his life, and then let us read his last will and testament. In different fashion, each will give us insight into his calm, unhasting life.

It was a spring morning in the year A.D. 28. Jesus was on the shores of the Sea of Galilee, and the crowd which milled around him was so vast that the only way he could address them and be heard was to get into a boat and speak to them from the lake. He spoke—as his custom was—in parables. Speaking in the open air to a great crowd calls for much exertion, but speaking from a boat across the water to people spread all along the shore would have completely exhausted most men. He went for his midday meal to Peter's house, and his disciples, glad to have him to themselves for a while, questioned him through the afternoon on the inner meaning of the things he had said to the crowd. After that he had another session with the people in the open air and told them more parables, but by evening he asked his men to get the boat out again as he wanted to go to the farther side of the lake. Peter did not care for the look of the sky, but they went. Other boats went too.

Tired by now, Jesus made himself comfortable on a cushion in the stern of the boat and dropped off to sleep.

Then the storm burst on them. His friends were used enough to storms on Galilee and could handle a boat with anyone, but this was no ordinary storm. The boat rolled and pitched and finally began to ship water. Meanwhile Jesus slept calmly on. The boat almost rolled over, but nothing disturbed him. It was indeed a parable of all his life. Nothing disturbed him!—but people's sin. He was in his Father's hands, and that was a place of total security. "God has the whole wide world in his hands." So he slept on.

It was his friends who could stand it no longer. When the boat had shipped so much water that it seemed almost to be filling, they woke him up in terror and said: "Master, don't you care that we are drowning?"

He woke up, stayed the wind, and said to the heaving sea, "Be still!" And it was still!

But the storm had driven the boat off its course. After his full day and broken night, Jesus stepped ashore, therefore, at an old graveyard where the crude Gadarene people lived; and immediately the most fearful bloodcurdling yells fell upon his ears. The next moment a naked madman rushed toward him. The poor fellow had broken pieces of chain still hanging on his wrists and ankles, and his body was lacerated with many wounds. Jesus remained as perfectly composed in this hurricane on land as in the storm at sea. With a calm clear word he cured the poor lunatic, but subsequent events unhappily struck such awe and perplexity into the minds of the people of the district that they pleaded with him to leave the area altogether. So he went back to the boat and crossed the lake again.

Another vast crowd was awaiting him. He was hardly ashore when a man of some position pushed his way through the crowd and begged him to come at once and heal his dying daughter.

"Why, yes," he said, "of course I'll come." The crowd swirled on all sides and it was difficult to get along. Moreover, in the crowd there was a poor woman who had suffered with a distressing hemorrhage for twelve years. It was her sickness that had made her poor. She had spent all she had in seeking a cure. But now she had such faith in Jesus that she felt, "If only I could touch his clothes, I'd be better," and in that utter faith she just touched his outer garment as he passed and felt at once that she was healed.

But Jesus stopped. He knew in some strange way when his healing power had been drawn on. He stopped! "Who touched my clothes?" he said. The question seemed silly with hundreds of people milling around. Moreover, the father of the dying little girl was almost frantic with fear and haste. But Jesus calmly stood and looked around until the poor woman stumbled forward and told him everything. He gave her a lovely blessing, but he was still speaking to her when a messenger broke through to say that the girl was dead. "It's all over," he said. "Don't come any farther."

Jesus looked at the heartbroken father and murmured: "Take no notice of that. Just go on believing."

So off he went again and finally got to the house. It was pandemonium. There was quite a crowd there, sobbing and screaming. Jesus put them all out. He did it in his own calm way, but he was quite firm. They found themselves outside. He went into the death chamber with only the mother and father and three of his friends, and taking hold of the little girl's hand, he said, "Little darling, get up!" And she got up! Turning to her mother, Jesus said with a smile: "Just give her something to eat!"

That gives us a little idea of *some* of the events of two typical days. There he is, handling great crowds, schooling his men in private, weathering a wild storm, encountering a madman, healing the sick, raising the dead . . . on and on he goes for three years *of unbroken peace.* "Toil, unsevered from tranquillity." Never breathless. Never hurried. All quiet within.

Is it any wonder, then, that the only thing he mentions in his last will and testament is his unearthly peace? He had a robe to leave, but he never mentioned his robe in his will. Almost the last thing he saw with clear eyes from the cross were the soldiers dicing for his robe. But his will was all about his peace. This was his treasure. This was his greatest gift. Joy you cannot always have, but always you can have peace. Peace in the Father's hands. Peace in the Father's will. Peace in the mind's deep core.

"Peace I leave with you, my peace I give unto you: not as the world giveth, give I unto you. Let not your heart be troubled, neither let it be afraid."

What would it be worth to you to have his peace in your mind?

Have this mind in you, which was also in Christ Jesus. (*A.S.V.*)

TO SUM UP

We are made with a heartache nothing on earth can satisfy—not even health, wealth, and human love.

Only God can give us peace of heart and mind.

Christ had perfect peace of heart and mind.

He was under enormous pressure of work, and he had enemies bent on destroying his life and his mission.

Yet he lived in perfect peace and died bequeathing his peace to his friends.

14

WHY DO I FEEL INFERIOR?

DURING the last thirty years, few phrases have become more common on the borderlands of medicine and psychology than "the inferiority complex." There is no doubt that the term has been overused and misused. Some people who have claimed to suffer from it did not clearly know what it was. Dr. Adler—the first to give the term currency—has been at pains to point out that in some circumstances a sense of inferiority can be an advantage in life and a great spur to ambition. He once concluded a lecture by saying, "I wish you all a creative inferiority feeling."

Nevertheless, an inferiority complex, in the proper sense of the term, is real and awful. Though it normally develops in childhood and youth, it can blight a whole long life. At its worst, it can develop into a deep self-hate.

The home and the school are often the greenhouse which quickens the seed of self-despising in the soil of a child's mind. Parents—even good parents—sometimes give their children the idea that they love them *for* something: if they are very good, if they are very clever, if they work very hard. The parents may have made sacrifices for the child's education. They may themselves be able, resolute, and admirable people. To the superiority of their years and experience is added in the child's mind the weight of their worth in character and the memory of their sacrifices so willingly made.

But a genius could barely live up to this towering expectation—and their son grows aware with passing time that he is no genius. Moreover, he has his naughty periods, and there are work-times when he wants to play. The thought comes to him that he is falling below their just anticipation. The conviction deepens that he does not make the grade. He begins to despise himself. If, with school past, he has a couple of failures and perhaps an unhappy love affair, he can become a chronic case of self-hate and a secret martyr to inward loathing.

Or a little girl may find herself in a broken or loveless home. She may become aware while still very young that "she ought to have been a boy," that her sex had disappointed her parents and her advances in love are rebuffed. If, with a chill already striking at her heart, she is mishandled at school, the honest and desolating conviction may grow in her that she is an odd and quite unattractive person; and she will react to the world awkwardly and foster self-despisings within.

It would surprise the self-satisfied to discover what blind hatred and secret contempt some people have for their own nature. To spite themselves they exaggerate the marvelous gifts of other people. They look on their neighbor through rose-colored spectacles and at themselves through the darkest blue. They see their rivals as supermen and superwomen, and spurn the stirrings within them of the gifts they unquestionably have.

They are mistaken in both their attitudes. Their neighbors are not the dazzling geniuses their own self-hate would suggest, and their personal gifts are capable of a development which would be rich in service in the circles where they move.

But while this inbuilt conviction remains that they are misshapen in nature and clearly below the grade, their personality suffers partial paralysis and the community loses the work they might otherwise have done.

Self-hate does not always parade itself as self-hate. It is one of the quirks of the inferiority complex that it often assumes the manner of superiority. Men strut and strike an attitude. Women talk louder and longer. Neither have the dignity and repose of the fully integrated personality. This strutting and noisiness *could* be pride and self-importance! But it is often a disguise of those secret self-despisings which we have been examining—the blatant effort of the will to talk oneself out of conscious littleness and make a bid for the stature a man fears he does not possess. The pose and the noise are calculated to cover self-contempt in the soul.

It will be clear, then, that this secret self-despising *could* be regarded as the opposite of pride and self-glorification—and up to a point this is true.

But only up to a point! The opposite of pride (as we have seen) is humility, and inferiority must never be confused with humility. Some devotional books confuse the two and seem almost to encourage a man to despise himself. But this is a deviation from Bible teaching.

The Bible (as we have seen) teaches a proper self-love. "Thou shalt love thy neighbor *as thyself*." If I am truly despicable and to be treated only with contempt, so, doubtless, is my neighbor, and why should I love him?

God answered all this quibbling when he died on the cross. However little worth there may be in us by nature, he put worth upon us by dying for our salvation. No man is to be despised (even by himself) who was so dear to God that He shed the sacred blood.

When Muretus, the poor scholar, was overtaken by sudden sickness centuries ago in the Low Countries, he was picked up out of the gutter and carried into a hospital. It never crossed the mind of the two young surgeons standing by the table on which he had been laid that this mud-stained ill-clad boor could understand a word of their conversation, for they were talking in Latin. The theme of their discussion was a certain dangerous operation which was just being mooted in Europe, and with a sudden inspiration, one of the surgeons nodded toward Muretus and said to his colleague: "Shall we try the experiment on this worthless creature?"

But Muretus had understood every word. Who better? Nor did he say, "I am a scholar and a gentleman. You can't do that to me!" In polished Latin he said to those startled youths: "Will you call that man 'worthless' for whom Christ died?"

That is the ground of our worth: the solid, sufficient, and only basis of it. *And it is the same for everyone.* We were dear enough to have shed the sacred blood. That truth, grasped by the mind and held in the heart, could heal us of our self-despisings. Nor does God love us *for* anything—because we are good, or clever, or industrious. He loves us for ourselves alone. Why, then, should we torture ourselves? If pride is a sin, is not self-respect a duty? If we cannot love ourselves, cannot we at least be friendly and kind?

Get your sins forgiven and find the way to self-respect. To realize yourself as a child of God is to have a quiet dignity which is beautifully independent of class, education, rank, and wealth.

You can see it most clearly in Jesus Christ. Let us look at ourselves again in his mirror. Having faced in our own minds the inferiorities and self-despisings from which we may suffer, let us look into that ineffable mind, perfectly knit and splendidly whole.

Having found nothing of pride in him, we find nothing of inferiority either. The opposite of inferiority is a balanced unified personality—and such harmony in the soul expresses itself in an unforced dignity which is as far from pompousness as it is from servility. It neither cringes nor struts. It is beyond patronage. Those who have it move among their fellows as kings.

Jesus—as we should expect—had it supremely. Men called him a carpenter, and we know he was humble, but what an unearthly dignity rested on that human form! Turn the pages of the Gospels and notice it again and again.

Three things may be commonly supposed to test the dignity of any man.

First: familiar intercourse with other people. No dignity, it is said, can survive that. Common sayings express that old conviction: "Familiarity breeds contempt." "No man is a hero to his valet."

Second: the awful majesty of the law. Few people can come to the bar of justice, set out with all the panoply of state, and face a capital charge *with serenity*. The most assured dignity has been known to quail before that.

Third: contact with military might. To a mind essentially gentle and civilian, there is something deeply repugnant in naked force. Not much dignity can survive in a man hauled off by a posse of soldiers.

Now it happens that we can see Jesus in each of those situations. Was he ever cheap? Did he ever cringe? Is he, at any moment, servile?

Search the Gospels from end to end and you will never find that those closest to him ever took liberties with him. The very conditions of the common life of Jesus and his friends necessitated the closest intimacy. He had no private apartments into which to withdraw. He had no apartment at all. He ate and drank with them, traveled and slept with them, washed and worked with them . . . but they never took liberties with him. Always—though he was a Galilean as they were, talked in their accent, and had hands hard with toil—they held him in reverential awe. They enjoyed his friendship, but they knew he was apart. They were intimate but not familiar; in his heart, yet at his feet. Indeed, there were times when their awe of him prevented their asking or answering questions. Mark tells us that when He led them up to Jerusalem on the last journey, they followed but they were afraid. Too afraid, it seems, to ask questions. He tells us also that when they had been arguing among themselves as to which of them should be greatest, and He asked them afterwards what the discussion had been about, they were ashamed to tell him.

What unearthly presence was this that kept them dumb? Clearly, he was of their own kind and clearly he was apart.

No man a hero to his valet? But these were the very men (Jews to a man, with the oneness of God built into the structure of their thinking) who first proclaimed to the world that He was God incarnate. They knew him in all the testing intimacies of daily life, but they became so sure of his person that most of them died for the faith that he was God himself.

Or see him at the judgment seat of Pilate. The Romans (and Pilate in particular) had a special contempt for Jews. And when Pilate took his place at the judgment seat on that never-to-be-forgotten day, it was just a routine job. Another Jew to try on a ridiculous but capital charge.

And then Jesus came in! He was stained with the blood of the garden. His garments were awry. There was a wale across his face where he had been struck. But there was a dignity about his person which almost knocked the procurator dumb. He tried to get him released. When he failed, he allowed our Lord to be scourged, and the soldiers put a purple robe on him and forced a crown of thorns upon his head. They spat on him and struck him with their hands.

And that was how Pilate saw him for the last time: with the spittle on him, and the blood of the pillar and the garden, and thorns round his forehead; with a purple robe dragged round him to mock his royal state; with all hell let loose and the Son of God *burlesqued.*

And as Pilate looked at him, it was not the robe he saw, nor the spittle, nor the blood, nor the thorns, but a kingly figure, noble, majestic, dignified, regal, shining . . . and (the Bible says) *"he was the more afraid."*

Or see him in his contacts with the military. When the soldiers first came to arrest him in the garden, he responded immediately to his name. He walked toward them saying, "I am he!" and as he did so, unarmed and unresisting, they (with their weapons in their hands) retreated before him *"and fell to the ground."* What unearthly dignity was this that armed men fell back before it?

It was a soldier who broke the awful silence which followed his last great cry from the cross. The centurion had seen it all and heard it all. It was utterly unlike anything he had seen or heard before. As the breath left His body and the scarred flesh hung limply on the cross, he said in an awed voice: "He must, indeed, have been a son of God!"

There it is! You so secretly inferior, inwardly unsure, consciously unequal. He so whole, so dignified, so completely the master of every situation.

"But I can't be like *that!*" you say. "He was the Son of God."

He will make *you* a son of God: not a servant only but a *son,* a joint heir with himself. That ought to end inferiority! That should root out the self-despisings from your mind!

And notice the skill with which he transforms your mind and secures you from the abyss of pride on the one side and the pit of inferiority on the other. Your dignity arises solely from your relationship to him. How can the child of a King feel inferior? How can a blood-bought sinner be proud?

Have this mind in you, which was also in Christ Jesus. (*A.S.V.*)

TO SUM UP

Many people feel inferior and some even hate themselves.

No Christian should feel inferior. He is a child of a King and dear enough to have shed the sacred blood.

Christ displayed no inferiority.

Indeed, his dignity was such that—

His intimates took no liberties.

His judge feared Him as he condemned Him.

Armed men were awed by his presence.

He could root out inferiority from *you.*

15

CAN I HOPE TO BE FREE OF FEAR?

It may be said without hesitation that all human beings are subject to fear. There are senses in which it is natural and good that it should be so. Not all fear is craven and harmful.

Fear in the form of caution has been one of man's stoutest allies in the long development of our race. It has made man careful in his dealings with wild beasts, in his contact with other tribes, and in all his ventures into the unknown. It still plays a not-unimportant part in modern life in this cautionary role. Common as road accidents are in the modern world, they would be enormously increased but for fear.

Fear, moreover, is a guardian of morality. In primitive times it took the form of taboo. In modern times men dread the loss of health. Many men, away at the war, were kept in the paths of decency by the fear of a foul disease. A teacher of ethics would say that the motive was a poor one; but most tempted men, back in the security of home, are grateful for the fear that built a wall between themselves and their follies.

Fear has moved man to some of the greatest discoveries he ever made. Fear of the dark led him to make the candle, the oil lamp, and the electric light. Fear of pain pressed him on to the discovery of anesthetics. Fear of disease drove him to discover or devise the healing drugs.

Unhappily, however, fear does not keep to its beneficent role. Fear (as the Bible says) has *torment*. It overreaches itself. It has become one of the major maladies of mankind.

People are tortured by fear. It seems to have infected all life with dreadful apprehension. There seems nothing into which fear cannot intrude with desolating consequences.

People fear failure and (sometimes even!) success. They fear the past and fear the future. They fear poverty, ill health, disgrace, and disaster. They fear something; they fear nothing. The tangible and intangible can both inspire dread. They fear passing time, loss of youth, the hurt of waning powers, pain, and bereavement. People fear for themselves and fear for their dear ones. Cancer and insanity are enormous bogies in the minds of millions. They dread dying, death, and after death. They even fear God—not with that awesome filial fear which is seemly in mortals in contact with Deity—but with an appalling dread as one whose punishments are vindictive and inescapable.

Finally they come to fear fear itself, so it can stalk through life like a ghostly nameless specter attaching itself to nothing in particular and casting its gloom over the sunniest days. Said Montaigne: "I fear nothing but fear" . . . and myriads would say it with him.

Moreover, it belongs to the sinister nature of fear that it drags a man to the very thing he dreads. Job said: "That which I feared has come upon me . . ." and many would want to add, "and *because* he feared." Nor does our fear remain in the mind. It scars the body. It heightens the blood pressure, weakens the heart, and plants ulcers where we digest our food. It throws the body right open to any evil germ which is about. An Eastern legend says that a pilgrim met the Plague and asked, "Where are you going?" The Plague replied: "I am going to Baghdad to kill five thousand people." A few days later the pilgrim met the Plague again and charged him with killing fifty thousand instead of five thousand. "Oh, no!" said the Plague, "I killed only five thousand; the others died of fear."

When fear really takes grip of a human mind, it can distort the loveliest things and, by some twisted logic, turn even the truth against itself. A doctor was talking to a new patient the other day. In great alarm the patient mentioned a rare and deadly disease of the liver and claimed to be suffering from it. "Nonsense!" protested the doctor. "You are not suffering from that. In fact, you wouldn't know whether you had it or not. It is a disease which gives no discomfort at all."

"That's just it!" gasped the poor patient. "My last doctor told me that. That is how I know I have it. I feel quite well!"

Who can deliver us from fear? Who ever lived without it, in its dangerous and exaggerated forms?

It is no good saying that *all* fears are groundless. The shallow pertness of optimism ("Cheer up, it may never happen") is powerless against the deeper fears. Age, waning powers, bereavement, death . . .

they belong to the very nature of this mortal life and they will surely come.

Is it true that our Lord lived free of every foolish fear? Had he such complete trust in his Father's love and power that (with mounting wickedness all around him) he could go on without the disablement of fear?

Let us look again into the mirror of his peerless life and see if there was fulfilled in him the Bible promise: perfect love casts out fear.

It is important that we remember at this point that Jesus lived in *our* world. The whole meaning of God taking our flesh is that we should learn what God is like, and how the life of God can be lived in *our* world. It was a world of sickness and suffering, of wickedness and hate. It was a world of accident, earthquake, and famine; a world of treachery, lust, and war. Jesus knew how parents could fear for their children and how children could fear for themselves. Lunacy was common in the world where Jesus moved, and death was not always gentle and in bed. Crucifixion was common in the days of Jesus. He must often have seen a young man dying in slow agony upon a cross.

Nevertheless, he was insistent in his teaching that fear (properly understood) had only one Object. He told his friends that they were to fear God: *only* God. "I will tell you whom you ought to fear. Fear him who is able to cast both soul and body into hell." Yet, even so, it is not to be a fear "that has torment." It is the awed and fitting fear of a mortal for his God. It is filial and trusting. It includes the "deepest, tenderest fears." For the rest, they were to fear nothing. One of his favorite phrases was "Fear not!" Again and again it rang out. "Fear not!"

And what he preached, he lived. Gethsemane apart (and that needs special study), he does not seem aware of disabling fear. And the hidden secret of Gethsemane is not fear. Dealing with angry mobs or angry madmen, in storm at sea or meeting the concentrated hate of his enemies ashore, he is never afraid. Facing the cross itself, he calls out to his men: "Let not your heart be troubled, neither let it be afraid."

Picture him on one occasion when a mob turned ugly. He had been back to his old home town of Nazareth and preached in the synagogue a sermon so offensive to his hearers that the people rose against him and drove him, not only out of the synagogue, but out of the city. Indeed, they brought him to a cliff edge high above their town with the intention of throwing him over.

There is no trace of fear in his demeanor throughout the whole incident. He was plainly aware of the provoking character of what he said, and pressed the point home with such sharpness that no one could miss it. Nor could it be said afterward that he had not made the truth plain to them all.

When they rushed upon him with murder in their hearts, he remained the same calm fearless leader his friends in Capernaum knew him to be. From the very brow of the hill, he turned aside with dauntless dignity and passed unharmed through their midst.

Inevitably the question arises in our mind: "How was Christ able, living dangerously as he did, to keep free of tormenting fear; and how was he honestly capable, in a world honeycombed with hazards, to urge others not to be afraid?"

Clearly, he did not do it like "optimists" do it: denying plain impending perils; turning a blind eye to unpleasant facts; persisting in looking on the bright side of the accounts right up to the morning when the receiver comes in; kidding themselves that nothing is harmful if they do not *think* it is; assuring people, against all the evidence, that what they fear will not happen. Jesus said plainly to his friends: "In the world you will have tribulation."

Just as clearly, he did not advise his friends to pray for deliverance from this world of tribulation. He said to his Father of his friends: "I pray not that thou shouldest take them out of the world, but that thou shouldest keep them from evil."

His own utter fearlessness, and the ground of his clarion call to others not to fear, was his complete confidence that his Father was on the throne and that all his Father's purposes were loving, wise, and good. Being assured of that, how could he fear? Infinite wisdom and infinite love were over and behind all things. Fear nothing, therefore! The most diabolical machinations of evil are powerless against the throne of God. To timorous mortals Christ would say:

What though thou rulest not?
Yet heaven, and earth, and hell
Proclaim: God sitteth on the throne,
And ruleth all things well!

The second ground of Christ's fearlessness was his confidence that his Father could turn all the "disasters" of life into spiritual success. He could wrest not only the wrath of man but the sin of man to his own divine ends. In the face of the most awful things that could happen, Jesus affirmed: "If my Father allows this, it is good unto me!" To see that clearly in the last testing hours of his life, he wrestled into a bloody sweat in Gethsemane . . . but he saw it. Calm and serene again, he declared: "The cup *which my Father hath given me,* shall I not drink it?" The cross on which he died proclaims the truth of his insight to all the world.

It was sin at its foulest; it was love at its purest. It was earth's worst; it was heaven's best. It was man's lowest; it was God's highest. Jesus knew that his Father—great in creation—was great in transformation too. Hence he could look the darkest probabilities in the face—and not be afraid. Filled with trust and holy love, his mind had no crevices for fear. Nor—if his mind were in us—should we.

> When 'tis deeply rooted here,
> Perfect love shall cast out fear;
> Fear doth servile spirits bind;
> Jesus is a noble mind.

Have this mind in you, which was also in Christ Jesus. (A.S.V.)

TO SUM UP

Fear is in all men and women.
Some of it is good.
But much of it is evil and tormenting.
Christ was free of all tormenting fear.
He was free of fear because he was convinced that:

1. His Father was on the throne and all his purposes were loving.
2. His Father could turn even evil to good.

16

HOW CAN I GET RID OF RESENTMENT?

ONE of the most virulent germs which can attack the human mind is resentment, and it is all the more dangerous because it often does its deadly work without being isolated and recognized for what it is. It is one of the most evil things in the world. The harmonious working of communal life at all levels depends on right relationships, and resentment is the enemy of these. It poisons the relations between man and man, woman and woman, husband and wife, class and class, church and church, nation and nation. It is resentment which often inflames the other causes which lead to war. Resentment has its part in buttressing the barriers between denominations and hindering the reunion of Christ's church. The pride of the wealthy, the privileged, and the "highborn" in all societies has been answered in the long-burning resentment of the people they "lorded" it over. The art of living together will never be mastered till resentment is mastered too.

Nor are the ravages of this germ less obvious in the individual mind. It breeds bitterness, depression, and disease. It causes nervous breakdowns and mental unbalance. It kills joy and fosters self-pity. The good that would come to the world if resentment were banished is beyond computation.

The reason why it is hard at times to isolate and recognize resentment as an evil thing is because it is so skillful in justifying itself. People think that if resentment is justified they may *legitimately* hold it; that they *ought* to hold it; that it would be foolish and weak *not* to hold it; that if a man's reputation were taken away, say, by the evil slanders of an enemy and the man did not resent it, he would be a worm and no man.

It is not the naturalness of resentment that is the most important thing, but the *poisonous nature of the emotion*. Legitimate or not, it is an evil germ inside the mind, and that evil germ is in the mind of the man who entertains it, not in the mind of the man who caused it. However damaging slander may be to a good man's reputation and however concerned he *must* be to correct the harm that is done, if he harbors resentment of the injury over the years, the resentment will do him more harm than the slander. It will eat away his peace of mind and shadow his home. A man made bitter and hateful by some great injury might fairly protest that he had a lot to make him so, but would that really be a compensation to a mature mind? Would it be a compensation to those he lived with?

I knew a man years ago whose young and lovely wife was killed by a drunken motorist. That desolate man was left to face the world alone with twin children—a boy and a girl. That he should be broken in sorrow for a while everybody understood, but when the shock had passed and the edge had come off his grief, he burned with a concentrated hate against his wife's murderer. Always (and not without justification) he referred to the drunken motorist as the "murderer."

His home grew dark and darker. He became a sullen recluse. The children felt that they had lost not only their mother but their father. And they had! There are senses in which he had died as much as his wife had done, but there lived in his place a morose monster of whom the children grew half afraid. And he maintained his concentrated hate out of some twisted loyalty to his wife's memory and on the ground (which no one dare deny) that his resentment was justified.

There was no cure for that much-injured man, and no recovery of his health, and no happiness for his motherless children until he came to the point of forgiveness and sought the healing of his awful sorrow in God.

But resentment is not always, or often, as plain as that; and it is seldom so excusable. Most of the injuries which wounded human nature nurses as "justification" for resentment are exaggerated and some of them are entirely fanciful. People will "hold" against their neighbors things of which their neighbors were never guilty. They will put a full credence on something which someone was supposed to have said and guard it like a rotten tooth which frankness and boldness could have drawn in five minutes. Firmly cupped in the gum, it aches intermittently through the years and infects every mouthful they chew. Resoluteness could have cleared the misunderstanding up in moments. The neighbor never said that at all. He said *this*. It is not the same thing. This grievance illustrates, not *his* barbed tongue, but *your* touchy nature. If there *was* an element of truth in the suspicion, would it not have been better for your peace of mind to dismiss it with magnanimity? Could anything else establish so clearly your own mental maturity? But like a silly child, you have remembered it through the years *to your own hurt*. Fancy a man *cultivating* the virus of influenza in his own body! But he would be less a fool than the man who cultivates the germ of resentment in his own mind.

Is it not clear, then, that the robe of justification with which resentment normally seeks to clothe itself is a disguise? It is *not* justified. It is begotten often of false information out of oversensitiveness. We imagine and exaggerate things, and when we dress up our imaginings and exaggerations in the robes of righteousness, we are falsifying the facts. It is often done, of course, at the subconscious level of our minds. The disguise is used to get the nasty thing past our consciences. It allows us to wallow in our dislikes with a sense of justification.

But we pay a big price for that kind of wallowing. Justified or unjustified, resentment is deadly, deadly to inner happiness, quiet content, and health of mind.

What, then, can we do about resentment? We cannot wisely suppress it. Driven underground, it will only store up trouble for later on. It is not much better to be constantly talking about it. It often renews itself in the telling. To make it a major motive in life and deliberately to plan revenge is perhaps the foulest, most foolish thing of all.

We ought to look again at the mirror of Christ. He was gloriously free of resentment and gave many hints of how it may be overcome. In his teaching, and still more in his example, we shall learn how to banish this evil thing from our minds.

Jesus always advised people to settle their differences at once. He said: "Agree with thine adversary quickly." He knew the danger of the feud, and how resentment can burn in a man's heart for years, and how the bitterness of one family toward another can be left like a legacy to succeeding generations. The Capulets and Montagues are found among all people. He said in effect: "Clear these differences up immediately."

Yet he knew also how resentment (like jealousy) can often flame against our own kin. Piety and sacrifice are unacceptable to God, he said, if there is resentment in the heart. "If, while you are offering your gift at the altar, you should remember that your brother has something against you, you must leave your gift there before the altar and go away. Make your peace with your brother first, and then come and offer your gift."

Moreover, Jesus was able to hate the things which people did—and love the people at the same time. How he must have loathed, with his inconceivable sensitivity of soul, the bestiality of publicans and the shameless soliciting of harlots! Yet he loved them so dearly and sought them so persistently that when his enemies labeled him a "friend of publicans and sinners," he could not deny it. It is here that so many "good" people fail. Their detestation of certain conduct becomes detestation of the people whose conduct it is. Though they are often wholly unaware of it, they may half-envy the license of the people they ferociously condemn, and moral condemnation mingled with envy produces resentment in their hearts.

Furthermore, Jesus had the power to see the good in the worst, and that is a great barrier built against hate and resentment. Though this story is not in the Bible (and comes to us from a Persian source), it could easily be true of the founder of Christianity. Jesus came one evening to the gate of a certain city and sent his disciples ahead to prepare the evening meal. He himself was drawn to a crowd in a corner of the marketplace. They were gathered around a dead dog. The poor beast lay in the gutter with a rope around its neck. Perhaps, only those who have traveled in the East can imagine the sight. The emaciated body, the sores, the filth, the stomach. . . . One by one, the members of the crowd made their comment. "Filthy beast!" said one. "Clearly hung for stealing," said another. "It poisons the air," said a third. "What a repulsive sight!" remarked a fourth. Then Jesus spoke. In a momentary quietness he murmured: "Pearls were not whiter than those teeth!"

The ability to see the good in those we dislike guards the heart from hate and the mind from resentment.

It also enabled Jesus to love men and women for what they *could* be. He had not only sight but insight. He saw people, not just as they were, but as God could make them. He even named them in confident expectation of the change! When he called the unstable Simon a

"Rock," He named the man who one day would appear. His loving faith "educated" the man.

To see the higher possibilities in people (even before they see them themselves) affects our attitude toward them and militates against our dislike.

Christ's teaching and example are nowhere more moving than when he came to die. The "first word from the cross" is among the sublimest words Jesus ever uttered. Tradition and the sense of the thing both indicate that this prayer leaped from his heart as they were actually nailing him to the cross. Prostrate on the wood still flat on the ground, he cried as the blood spurted from his palms: "Father, forgive them; for they know not what they do."

To concentrate on this single Gospel incident alone will teach us more of how to deal with resentment in our own minds than reading many volumes.

Notice, first, that *he forgave them*. He who had need that none should forgive him but who taught his friends to pray, "Forgive us our trespasses, *as* we forgive them that trespass against us," freely forgave. Nothing that happened on this amazing day would have surprised the soldiers as much as this. Rough men as they were, and used enough to crucifixions, always (I imagine) they expected a torrent of curses when the nails went home. But from this unearthly prisoner, not condemnation—but forgiveness!

Notice, secondly, *he prayed for them*. There is nothing like honest prayer to scour hate out of the heart. There was no hate in *his* heart. But his example is no less impressive to us whose hearts are not strange to resentment. "How can I get rid of my deep resentment toward the man who injured me?" people ask. Here is one way: pray for him.

Notice, in the third place, that *he made allowances for them*. Of whom was Christ thinking when he said, "They know not what they do"? Pilate? the people? the priests? the Pharisees? the soldiers? . . . Who can tell? Dare I raise the question and still be reverent: "Was it true?" Could it be said with exactness that they did not know what they were doing? Pilate knew He was innocent. So did the priests. The soldiers must have suspected it. The Pharisees were blinded by their own bigotry, and the people were willing to be fooled.

Of course, *they did not know who He was*. So it was *partly* true that they did not know what they were doing.

Therefore, he seizes on that! Mark the way in which magnanimity works! He spreads over the whole foul deed the kindly judgment of their ignorance and tells his Father in his death throes that this allowance must be made: "They know not what they do."

If only, at our lesser Calvaries, we could rise to this!—and say of that drunken motorist, for instance, "He did not know what he was doing"; of the man who slandered us (and did not fully realize how it injured our reputation); of the girl who stole that faithless husband's love (because she half-believed him when he said that he had never known love till he met her)—if only we could say with Christ's forgiveness and sincerity: "They know not what they do."

Notice, in the fourth place, that *he served them*. Their wickedness could not defeat his love. I believe that he was as free to walk away from the hill of Calvary as he was free to walk away from the cliff edge above Nazareth. He *accepted* death. He laid himself on the wood. He said in effect: "If you will do this to me, I can bear it." There was no other way to defeat sin. Sin and love were in decisive battle. If he drew back, sin won.

And victory remains with love:
For He, our Lord, is crucified.

So he served them in the midst of their hate. He was dying *for* them as well as *by* them. That they did not know that, and did not care, made no difference. He served them.

"How can I get this resentment out of my mind?" people ask again. Here is another way. Serve them! Thoughtfully, deliberately, prodigally, give yourselves to those you find it hard to love. Resentment recedes as service comes in.

Notice, finally, that *he loved them*. Amazing love is written all over the "place of the skull." He who had set Moses aside to say: "Love your *enemies*, and pray for them that persecute you" was consummating now a whole life lived on that principle.

Some Jewish scholars question that. They say that Christ's fierce denunciation of the Pharisees was a contradiction of his teaching that we were to love our enemies.

I cannot see the contradiction. His fierce invective was against their blind bigotry and an all-but-frantic effort to save people who could call the light darkness and come near to believing it themselves. And when he died on Calvary he died for the Pharisee as well as for the publican.

'Tis Love! 'tis Love! Thou diedst for me!
  I hear Thy whisper in my heart;
The morning breaks, the shadows flee,
  Pure, universal Love Thou art;
To me, to all, Thy mercies move:
Thy nature and Thy name is Love.

"But *I* cannot love like that!" the honest human heart will answer. "If that is the reply to resentment, it will elude me forever."

Not necessarily forever. If he *lives* in us—and it is *that* hope which is leading us on—he will *love* in us, and all the spirit of his first word from the cross can appear in our occupied hearts. We also can forgive injuries, pray for our enemies, make every allowance for their wickedness, serve them, and love them to the end.

The first ever to die for Christ was Stephen. He was unjustly murdered. Christ lived in him. His last words were a magnificent echo of Calvary. They stoned him to death. One by one the stones pounded the life from his body but could not batter his Lord from his mind. His last word was a prayer. He struggled to rise by the city wall and cried: "Lord, lay not this sin to their charge," and fell asleep in Jesus. He also had the mind which was in Christ.

Have this mind in you, which was in Christ Jesus.

TO SUM UP

Resentment is an evil germ in the mind.

It is hard to recognize as evil because it clothes itself in a sense of justification.

But—justified or not—it is still a poison, and *it is in the one who holds it.*

Jesus was free of resentment.

His first word from the cross shows how he dealt with the temptation to it.

He forgave them,
prayed for them,
made every allowance for them,
served them, and
loved them to the end.

17

JEALOUS? WHO? *ME*?

We turn to another major malady of our minds—jealousy, with which (for our present purposes) we shall identify envy too, though a fine distinction *can* be made between envy and jealousy. It is, without any doubt, one of the saddest sicknesses of our human minds and fruitful of enormous harm.

We may define this vice as pain, grief, or annoyance felt at the happiness, success, or fortune of another; displeasure or regret aroused by the superiority of another—plus a certain degree of malice or malignity and a desire to depreciate the person envied. It is a vice to which few are entirely strange and from which some people suffer all their lives.

It was the secret hurt you felt when somebody with whom you had matched yourself in thought or with whom others matched you, surpassed you or was considered to have surpassed you. It was the secret elation and gloating you found in your heart when he stumbled and fell. That was jealousy! It is deadly in its nature and can cast a long shadow over the whole of life.

It is a peculiar vice in some ways. Normally, it operates within groups, professions, and classes. The soldier is jealous of the soldier, the actor of the actor, the ecclesiastic of the ecclesiastic. The philosopher does not envy the pugilist his distinction, nor the pugilist the philosopher.

It is (as Chaucer remarked long ago) a vice which takes no pleasure in itself. A proud man can enjoy his pride and a covetous man delight in his hoardings, but a jealous man gets nothing out of jealousy but torment. How it scorches him to notice the success of his rival!

It is more common in middle age than in youth. The ambitious youth can see himself surpassed and not be envious. After all, he has *youth*. There are latent powers in him, he feels, which have yet to come to their fullness. But a middle-aged man who sees himself surpassed has lost his youth and doubts if any vastly larger powers are hidden in him. Envy can fall upon him, therefore, like a fever.

Envy can be met at all levels of life, but it is more common among professional people and those who are competing for popular favor in the world of entertainment and of sport. But no one is free from the possibility of it.

It is not normally directed against the people who would seem most to incite it: those who vastly outsoar us in ability and who, as strangers, might seem to have no particular claim on our regard. It is directed rather to those who *just* outsoar us; who compete in the same circle and for the same esteem we covet, and who are judged by others to be better than we are (though we positively know they are not!).

The local football player is not jealous of the nationally famous and professional goal-scorer. He modestly admits that the giant is a better player than he is. It is of someone else *on the same team* or on a neighboring team, with whom he has matched himself in his mind, of whom he feels jealous, and the loud praise of whom is as torture to his spirit.

The amateur actress in the little country town is not jealous of the leading ladies of the city stage. She admires and studies them. One of them, no doubt, is her model and heroine. She magnanimously concedes that these ladies are far ahead of her—and yet she is *not* jealous of them. It is of the little cat in her own amateur dramatic society, or the society in the neighboring town, of whom she feels jealous: the girl whom others (how can they be so blind?) commonly agree just surpasses her in charm and ability and is clearly the better actress of the two. How lovely it would be to hear that she had become a failure! How nice to keep that cutting from one of the local papers (they have a very good dramatic critic on that paper) in which it is half-hinted that her rival has either been overestimated or is "going off"!

Now that is how jealousy works! It does not leap a chasm; it gets into crevices. The people we do not know and who completely outshine us do not provoke us to this sin. It is the people whom we *do* know, who move in the same circle, and who just surpass us, who unconsciously set the trap into which we fall.

It explains why our friends and relatives can also be the focus of our jealousy. Our pride excuses our failure to excel people in other circles by assuring us that they had superior advantages or influential connections, but when it is someone in our own circle (or even in our own family), that excuse is no longer there; and being totally unwilling to admit that it was superior ability or harder work, we take refuge in suggesting that it was "luck" or that he is not so scrupulous in some ways as we are or that he has a rather vulgar way of pushing himself into the public eye. Consequently, we are trapped into jaundiced criticism of others, depreciate their obvious gifts, impute low motives to them, are constantly censorious, and lose half the joy of our own success because other people seem to get a larger share.

Let any man, therefore, eager to be on guard against this subtle vice, watch himself in his estimation of those who are doing the same work that he is doing, and doing it in the same circle. Let him mount a *double* guard over himself when he hears them praised—even though the praise may honestly sound extravagant to him. Saul's jealousy of David may already have been a spark in his heart before the women shouted, but it flared into flame at the feminine cry: "Saul has slain his thousands, but David his tens of thousands." The bitterness that arose from that comparison neither music nor his rival's magnanimity could charm away. A man loses a just joy in his own triumphs when he is enviously obsessed with the greater triumphs of others.

How childish it is! A little boy worried his poor parents for months for a bicycle, and when he got it one Christmas morning, he was happy *for an hour!* He leaped on it with joy and cycled off to show his friend . . . and came back miserable. When they inquired where his exuberance had gone, he said: "George has been given a bicycle too. It is a better one than mine. It has a three-speed gear." . . . One can forgive it in a child, but what kind of maturity has a man or woman reached who can go through life begrudging other people their happiness and success, and losing his own joy while he does it?

Discerning people have often noticed that it is easier to sympathize with our friends in their sorrows than exult with them over their successes. Envy complicates the one and not the other. We cannot envy their sorrows. Many find it hard not to envy their joy. A girl who hears that her friend has been disfigured in an accident can literally ache with sympathy for her. On the other hand, if she is unloved herself and she hears that her friend has won the affection of the handsome steady young man they have both secretly admired, she will offer her congratulations but she does not thrill as she offers them. Something chill seems to have struck inside her. Even her good wishes seem labored and "worked-up."

Nor does it seem any use to tell people that envy is usually derived from ignorance: that people of whom they are jealous often have to carry secret burdens of which they are totally unaware, and that—could they know all their rivals' circumstances—they would not be eager to exchange their lots.

The cure must run deeper than that. The disease is so penetrating and persuasive that only the divine Physician is fully equal to our need. It is to Christ that we must turn. Only those who have the mind of Christ can have a mind fortified against the vice of envy.

It needs hardly to be said there is no trace of this spirit in Jesus. Jealousy directed many a shaft at him. He sent no shaft of jealousy in return. How the Pharisees hated him for his success with the multitude! They also were teachers, but they could not "get the crowd." They said bitterly: "The world is gone after him." The priests were as envious as the Pharisees. Pilate saw through them. Mark says that Pilate knew that they had handed Christ over to him "out of envy" (R.S.V.).

But one can read his fiercest denunciation of the Pharisees and find no hint of envy beneath it: just the righteous anger of One who knew that the truth of God was being obscured.

The absence of envy in Jesus will not seem so wonderful to some people as the absence of pride. "Of whom had *he* to be envious?" they will inquire.

Of whom *might* he have been envious? Of those with a home of their own—a place to lay their head? Of those not hunted for their lives; with every word noted, discounted, twisted, to be used in evidence at their trials? . . . Of those who could spend their whole time in prayer? It would have been but human had he felt some envy of them.

But there is no trace! He meets us in this dilemma of our sinful nature as in every other, holds up the mirror of his matchless mind that we may see ourselves as we are—and ourselves as we might be—and lets us know that he can turn the one into the other.

Can we glimpse the method by which he might bring us to release?

He is able, first, to make us *face* this sickness in our soul. That in itself is an essential condition of our cure. People can live for half a lifetime in honest ignorance that they are suffering from it. If they suspect it, they shrink from it. It is humiliating to admit it, and pride rebels at the idea that I should be jealous of *him*. "Jealous? Me? *Of him?!*"

So we brush it aside with scorn and go on for a few more years denying the deadly thing which is eating us all the time.

Christ is able, in the second place, to guide our impulse toward comparisons into channels which are fruitful. Constantly comparing ourselves with other people can do great spiritual harm. If we conclude that we are better or abler than they are, we can be trapped into pride. If we conclude that we are less able and clearly below them, we can be trapped into inferiority or envy.

Yet the impulse toward comparison is strong in us all.

Christ draws it toward himself and says, in effect, "Compare yourself with me. Accept this as the standard. Claim the help I offer and work to this end." So comparison becomes spiritually fruitful, and the stumbling block is made a steppingstone.

In the third place, Christ is able to convince us that each one of us has a place in the plan of God and that his plan is best. Being convinced of that, we envy no one. We can only wish them well in the working out of God's plan for them. If I am sure that infinite wisdom and infinite love are guiding my onward course, how can I want to change places with others? "In his will is *my* peace."

The last recorded conversation between Jesus and Peter in John's Gospel finds Peter trifling with the wrong kind of comparison and unduly concerned about the destiny of John. "What about him, Lord?" he said.

Jesus replied: "What does that matter to you? Follow me yourself!"

To every envious soul, wanting to know why others should have things they do not have, Jesus would say: "What does it matter to you? Follow me yourself."

Furthermore, Christ would take from us the greedy eagerness for human praise which is the cause of so much jealousy. It is a diabetic thirst for admiration which leads many people into this sin. *They* want the crowd, the applause, and the flattery. That is how they come to envy the people who get it.

Christ would teach them to live independent of the praise of men. He would have them fix their gaze on God alone, and be elated at his smile though all the world despise them, and be heartsore at his frown though all the world should think them great.

"The Master praises. What are men?"

Finally, he would teach all those who triumph never deliberately to provoke jealousy in others. It is hard for human nature, as we have seen, not to be envious at the success of friends; and any man enjoying a high measure of it ought to carry it lightly and not stress his capacity to excel. Old friends should have particular care. His aim should be to emphasize the old equalities and not the new differences, and so help them by his honest regard that the fight with jealousy is won and the old affection does not die in their hearts.

And Christ will reinforce all his efforts in the mind of his Christian friends. If they allow their Lord to do it, he will teach those tempted to envy to pray for the one who might provoke it, to speak well of him, and to love him still. The battle is won in the mind, and to have the mind of Christ is to have the victory over all envy.

Have this mind in you, which was also in Christ Jesus. (A.S.V.)

TO SUM UP

Jealousy is a peculiar vice:
it turns in circles, gets into
cracks, is more common in middle
age than in youth, and yields
nothing but torment.
Its presence explains why it is easier to
"weep with those that weep"
than to "rejoice with those that rejoice."
Christ alone can cure it.
He drew it but he never felt it.
He can make men face it and conquer it.
The battle is in the mind.

18

AM I A WHINER?

SOME people whine their way through life. Their first reaction to anything is negative and disparaging. They are resolutely miserable and make other people miserable too. Indeed, so set upon misery are they that it seems to be the only thing they enjoy, and they resist any efforts to cheer them as though they were being robbed of their one bit of pleasure!

If these people claim to be Christian, inevitably they get Christianity a bad name. No one unfortunate enough to live near them or work with them could believe that Christianity was a spring of joy. They moan their way through life and tempt other people to wish them out of this world they find so unhappy and into an early grave.

It would be fair to admit that some people could claim with justification that they have a great deal to be miserable about, but the odd thing is that it is often those with the greatest trials who moan least and those with the lighter afflictions who are martyrs to self-pity.

When I was in San Francisco I passed the offices of Sam Harrison. Sam, as a soldier in the American army, was all but killed three weeks before the last war ended. His left arm was blown off near the shoulder, only two fingers survived on his right hand, and his right knee was smashed. Everybody but Sam was sure he was dying. His chums were sure. The surgeons at the field hospital were sure. But Sam wouldn't die. He fought back the screaming waves of pain and plowed through the dark days of awful despair, and somehow his courage moved everyone to do more than their utmost for him.

Something else helped him too. There floated up from his subconsciousness a boyhood memory of a boring afternoon when he had sat with the family out visiting and heard a roomful of adults waste a shining hour by talking of their imaginary ailments. "When I'm grown up," he vowed to himself, "no matter what happens, I won't pity myself or talk about it."

Well . . . it had happened, and the thought shaped itself in his mind: "Can I keep my vow? Shall I whine and complain and get everybody pitying me—and run away?—or shall I shut up about my pains and try to forget them in helping others?"

He took the "high road" and began the same day. He began to fling from his bed humorous banter, remembered jokes, fun, and good-humored raillery, till the other wounded men joined in as well; and courage, light, and hope came into the ward. Back in the States he foolishly begged his wife to divorce him as a helpless fragment of man, but she dismissed the suggestion with the scorn it deserved.

He was twenty-seven months in the hospital. He had thirty-three surgical operations. But he has been out years now, is head of a business he has built himself, and is full of infectious fun. He never moans, spends his Saturday afternoons cheering the men in the military hospital, and finds endless things to be thankful for. To see him sign his letters at the end of the day is an artistic delight. He pulls the letter in front of him, holds it firm with the four-inch stump at his left shoulder, signs it neatly in a pen held in the two fingers of his right hand, sticks his hat on his head, and limps smiling home.

No self-pity, no moans. Just quiet gratitude for numberless mercies and an iron resolution to go bravely on.

What has happened to these people who succumb to self-pity? How did they get there? Is it just a question of temperament again? Were they born melancholic and will they remain that way until they die? Are some people more prone to this debilitating weakness than others? Is there any kind of radical cure?

Sensitive people are more prone to this malady than others. Sensitivity is a precious thing in the community. Much of the important work of the world is done by sensitive, highly nervous people. Sensitivity and unselfishness produce pity and sympathy. Those who feel keenly within themselves can feel keenly for others. But sensitivity wed to self-centeredness begets this miserable self-pity, and self-pity makes men and women into moaners and dreary pests. When every allowance has been made for the testing experiences of life, it cannot be denied that those who succumb to this are cowardly and self-centered. It is neither brave nor fine to be constantly complaining of our personal distresses—especially when our self-engrossment makes us blind to the greater distresses of others. One visit to a hospital of the blind or permanently disabled ought to cure such melancholy self-preoccupation. Alas! It doesn't. A man or woman obsessed with self-pity can pass through the wards of the blind and the bedridden and begin again in half an hour to complain of trivialities. The whole set of their thinking, and the emotional tone of their life, is blue; and everything dipped into it comes out with the dye. The weather is too hot or too cold, too humid or too dry. When it is perfect, they can still be miserable. They murmur sadly, "We'll have to pay for this!" They study all events until they find a dark side. If they cannot find it, they invent it. Advertisements for patent medicine are poison to them. They have every disease described. At a birth they sigh over the troubles ahead of the helpless infant, and at a death they wonder who will pay the funeral expenses.

The tendency to exaggerate the annoyances of life into major tragedies is one of the commonest marks of this malady. I recall a woman on whom I called once and found her bordering on hysteria. Her agony was so acute that my mind raced at once to all the awful hurts of life. Her husband?—he was dead, or dying, or disgraced, or running off with another woman. One of the grandchildren?—pounded to death beneath a streetcar, or certified insane. It was none of these things. She had found moths in the spare blankets!

Nor does the vice end in these absurdities. It ends in the gravest spiritual risk. One of the dread things about self-pity is that it opens our life wide to temptation. People obsessed with their troubles and foolishly exaggerating them easily lapse into a "don't care" mood. People self-persuaded that life has dealt hardly with them are ready to ignore the moral rules and snatch at things they think they have been cheated of . . . and anything can happen then. A man or woman sorry for himself will entertain suggestions he would spurn in other moods, and a spasm of self-pity is the only explanation of the moral wreck of people who at other times would have been immovably strong.

"I was caught on the rebound and sorry for myself," a woman said to me the other day. "I felt I didn't care what happened. . . ." Her whole life has been blighted by the sin which got in through a mood of self-pity.

No one is armored against the assaults of temptation if he has this weakness in the soul. Few of us are entirely free of it. It may not be our settled state of mind so that we whine our way through life, but we have spasms of it; and powerfully tempted in such a spasm, we also could make wreck of most things we hold dear. That we have not done so already is more by the grace of God than our own strong wills. That we shall not do so in the future, let us look again at the life of Christ.

There is no trace of self-pity in Jesus Christ. When he told an ardent would-be disciple that he himself had no place to lay his head, it was not an invitation to sympathy but a frank intimation to the young man of what he was taking on. When, in the unspeakable agony of his dying, there broke from his parched lips the cry "I thirst," none but the unbelievably callous would find self-pity in it. The dying may ask for a drink without being accused of complaining.

When—deepest mystery of all—he confessed from the cross that he felt deserted—"My God, my God, why hast thou forsaken me?"—he was marking some awful sense of desolation in his soul, but I cannot find *self-pity* in it. What sin-bearing means, no mortal can hope to understand. The human eye cannot pierce the dark cloud which rolled over his soul in those moments, but as a sense of separation from God is ever the worst consequence of sin, may it not be that he who knew no sin entered into its experience and lost, for the only time in his incarnate life, the sense of his Father's nearness?

But it is not self-pity! Anyone who could overhear the most awful word from the cross and resolve it into the cowardly weakness we are considering here must be spiritually insensitive to a blasphemous degree.

Christ's freedom from self-pity is all the more wonderful as we think our way into the conditions of his life. At what stages of his human existence his divine mission unfolded itself within his own consciousness we do not fully understand, but it is clear he knew that the course he was taking would alienate all who were dear to him—friends, brothers, sisters, mother—and that the implacable hate of his enemies would secure his ignominious and agonizing death. The temptation to self-pity must have been enormous; his flesh and blood would surely recoil from such a role. But on he goes, steadily, resolutely, even gaily.

Jesus has been called "the Man of Sorrows," but no one sorry *for himself* could have attracted and won people as he did. His fascination must have been measureless. That working married men could have left all to follow him, that multitudes should flock around on every side, that publicans and harlots could conquer the abasing shame his purity created in them and still long for his company, that young men should run to him and honestly declare that they would follow him wherever he went, indicates an infinite attraction in which gaiety must have had its part.

Nobody wants a whiner at a wedding. One *has* to ask them sometimes, but you do not *want* them there. People wanted Jesus at a wedding. They asked him to their parties—and it *made* the party if he came. He had enchantment (John called it "glory"), made nicknames, had fun, and carried light wherever he went. Who could have guessed, in the love he evoked and the laughter he started, that he was consciously walking the road to public humiliation and a torturing death?

With Easter past, it was, I think, as a man of joy that they most remembered him: as one who had convinced them that the best name for God was Father; that God was all-loving; that he had everything in his hands; that nothing was too good to be true; that even in the midst of the world's tribulations they were to be of good cheer, for he had overcome the world.

Like everything else in his peerless character, it runs down at the last to the complete trust in his mind.

His mind was securely built on the certainty that God was there and God was love.

Let that be true and nothing else matters.

Even the hard disciplines of life can be accepted with courage if love can use them. To moan about them is surely mean and mistaken; it is dishonoring God by implying that he is mismanaging his world, and it makes life miserable for those around us.

Unselfishly to turn our sensitiveness to sympathy for others is to copy Christ in still another way. We radiate good cheer, thrust our shoulder under other people's burdens, and—so far from whining—we learn the secret of radiant personality and even bubble at times with joy.

The secret is in a mind entirely "stayed" on God.

Have this mind in you, which was also in Christ Jesus. (A.S.V.)

TO SUM UP

Some people whine their way through life; they are martyrs to self-pity.

Self-pity is the child of sensitiveness and self-centeredness; it moans, magnifies annoyances into tragedies, and exposes one to fierce temptations.

It spreads misery all around.

There was no self-pity in the mind of Christ.

Being certain of his Father's being and love, he went bravely and gaily on his way.

19

THEY CALL ME A "NO" MAN

WE all know what a "Yes" man is. He is spineless, and a fawner. He is so afraid of the great man over him that he seldom ventures an opinion of his own and never opposes the view of his chief. He says "Yes" to everything the big personality utters until, at the last, he has no personality of his own. He becomes a colorless cipher whose characteristic attitude is a cringe.

But more common in the community than "Yes" men are "No" men; the people who take a negative and opposed attitude to all things. Their first and instant reaction to any new idea, or new method, or new approach, is "No." They see difficulties like mountains and opportunities hardly at all. Their superiors and subordinates have both noticed the peculiarity in them; they have come to expect the same monotonous answer to anything: "No."

What makes these people so consistently negative?

It is sheer inertia in some cases—the inclination of human nature with youth past to have everything "stay put." Change is not welcomed. They have learned to love their rut. In any case, change is almost sure to involve more work—more work during the period of adjustment if not more work later on—and they do not want more work.

A new idea is almost an affront to them. It seems to imply a criticism (though none is necessarily intended) of their past performance. "Haven't I been doing a good job already?" they seem to say. "Leave well alone!" So juniors are checked, and seniors find them "touchy" and hard to get on with, and every new idea founders on the rock of their negativism.

But often this sad state of mind rests on something even more obdurate than the inertia of human nature. It is often built upon those other sad states of mind which we have already considered here. Fear, inferiority, jealousy, and self-pity lie beneath a great deal of negativism. They may be masked. A man may be honestly unaware of their presence himself or even that he is constantly negative in his attitude to life, but the deadly pessimism of his thinking wears ruts into his mind, and "No! no! no!" is almost a reflex action of all his thoughts. Does he fear for the security of his position? Or does he secretly suspect that new ideas and new methods come from superior minds and hate to admit (though he secretly believes it) that his mind is inferior? Is he a whiner in his soul and sure that everything is likely to turn out ill, so that while things *are* holding together he thinks it folly to disturb them?

Whatever the reason, the negative mind is known to us all. Some of us do not need to study it in others. With a little divine aid we can see it in ourselves.

Moreover, a man or woman who is in the grip of negativism can easily become what the pyschologist calls a "contrasuggestible." The man in the street calls it "cussedness." A contrasuggestible does not merely oppose what you suggest, but fights it and argues for the opposite. He does it so readily and consistently that it appears to be a fixed principle of his thinking to oppose whatever others bring forward. Often he loves argument for argument's sake. He faces life like one always on the defensive—and half-convinced that the best form of defense is attack. An element of pride is involved. He seems to say concerning anything which is proposed: "You can't put that over on *me*," and he argues for the contrary at once.

Shrewd people compelled to live or work with a contrasuggestible develop a simple technique for outwitting them. They suggest the thing they do *not* want in order to get what they *do*. Wise women married to a husband of this type have made this reversed method of getting their own way almost second nature. Their husbands are as happy as contrasuggestibles can ever be. They live in the illusion that they are ruling the roost and keeping the little lady where she ought to be. The little lady is happy too.

Many of his friends regarded Bernard Shaw as a classic contrasuggestible. He worked on the large scale. Whatever the public had a taste for, he attacked. Conan Doyle speaks of his "perverted pleasure" in opposing and ridiculing what others enjoyed, and finds in this "delight in opposing whatever anyone else approved" the key to his complex character.

Most of his contemporaries regarded Henry Irving as a great actor and a masterly interpreter of Shakespeare. Shaw poured bitter scorn on both ideas. When Irving's son invited Shaw to his father's funeral, Shaw replied: "If I were at Westminster, Henry Irving would turn in his grave, just as Shakespeare would turn in his grave were Henry Irving at Stratford."

When the nation was at war, Shaw preached the gospel of peace; but when the Tsar's peace proposals were at the Hague and others were speaking in their support, Shaw came into the open to prove that peace would be disastrous. "Do what you could, he was always against you."

Do what you can, they are always against you! That is the key to the character of the contrasuggestible. It is negativism turned militant. Different disorders of the mind (as we have seen) lead to this contrary attitude, and sometimes it is fear and sometimes it is jealousy; sometimes it is inferiority and sometimes wounded pride. But in the wide range of its effects—from the automatic and obstinate "No" of those secretly fearful of others (and seldom big enough to admit that they are wrong) to the militant opposition of those who are against everybody else—the community suffers in all kinds of ways, and none suffers more than the "No" man himself.

Is there a radical cure for this sickness of the soul? If these sufferers could see themselves in the mirror of Christ, how would their contrary minds appear even to themselves in the perfection of his?

The mind of Christ is gloriously positive. His teaching is not life-denying but life-affirming. To assert—as some do—that Christianity is a bundle of negations is to caricature the sweetest thing on earth.

Indeed, so wrong are those people who suggest that Christ was intolerant of everything which made glad the heart of man that we can assert without reservation that his only intolerance was sin. All his teaching and example cry aloud that life is good. His whole purpose in coming to earth, he declared, was that we might have life and have it to the full.

If it is argued—as, of course, it could be—that the New Testament has much to say about self-denial and that Christ plainly laid it down that no one could be his disciple who was unwilling to bear a cross, it must be insisted that self-denial in the New Testament is never an *end,* only a means. In the most famous passage where Jesus praises self-denial and commends the cross, he says that those who lose their lives *shall find them.* Finding, not losing, is the last word of Christianity. Indeed, in one place Jesus goes into the mathematics of it! Whatever you lose you will receive a hundredfold—and eternal life as well.

Some people think that this is bad ethics. "Virtue is its own reward," they say. Their quarrel is with the New Testament, not with me. The New Testament is full of rewards. Even the Beatitudes are a list of them. *But they are the right rewards.* That man is bold who thinks he can improve the New Testament. Discipline, denial, and self-control are all part of the Christian life because they are part of the way to holiness, but *happiness* is the sequel to holiness. Enjoyment, not asceticism, is the last word. In the final analysis the gospel is an offer and not a demand.

Scrutinize the teaching of Christ with this in mind and its positive affirmative character leaps to view.

Life is good, says Jesus, and can be full. "I came that you might have life and have it more abundantly: Ask, and you shall have; seek, and you shall find; knock, and it shall be opened to you." Life, as Jesus speaks of it, isn't a low groveling thing to be endured with what stoical courage we can muster, but something to enjoy and delight in. He does not see us just as the fruit of the sexual passion of our parents, but as children of God, who in the greatness of his love even shares with his creatures the joys of creation and gives us to know the bliss of begetting our kind. Not ours, therefore, to greet life with fear and timidity, say "No" to its offer, and set ourselves by twisted "principle" in grim opposition to our fellows, but ours to run out and embrace life and know with the beasts of the field and the birds of the air that the first thing about life is to enjoy it. "It is your Father's good pleasure," said Jesus, "to give you the kingdom."

"Give!" What a sovereign word that is in the New Testament! Overbrimming abundance is the offer. Christ said through Paul: "All things are yours." Christ said through John: "Be faithful unto death, and I will *give* you the crown of life." (R.S.V.) Nor is any limit to be put to the "all things" he offers. All, all is yours. At the last, the meek *inherit the earth.*

Nor is life only good and full. It is free also.

So far from negativism and privation being characteristic of the life Christ offers, it is liberty of a quality the world cannot know. The core of Christ's teaching here is that we must bow to God and ultimately to him alone. Other authority can be legitimate in its subordinate place, but it is secondary and derived; and if conflict occurs, it must be disregarded for the divine authority. Hence, so far from the Christian man's being (as some people believe) imprisoned in law, he is in a deep sense a "law-less" man. Paul says so again and again; and he is not "law-less," of course, in the sense that he breaks the moral law, but that, having the mind of Christ, he outsoars the law's poor limits and does not need to be made to keep it. Those in whom Christ dwells are not *compelled* to keep the moral law; they *want* to. "For freedom did Christ set us free!" (A.S.V.) "Where the Spirit of the Lord is, there is freedom." (R.S.V.) "As free . . . but as bondservants of God." (A.S.V.) "If therefore the Son shall make you free, ye shall be free indeed." (A.S.V.)

Finally, this good, full, free life mounts to a bliss that is not really of earth at all. "Pleasure" is far too earthy a word to describe it. "Happiness" is better and "joy" is better still, but they both fail in adequacy. "Blessedness" is the supreme New Testament word, and "glory" carries it to heaven.

The testimony of those who have tasted all the dear delights of earth, yet know Christ too, is that no rapture can compare with the rapture of real religion.

> The love of Jesus, what it is
> None but His loved ones know.

Is glory only for heaven? Well . . . something of glory falls on the saints as they tread this earthly way.

> The men of grace have found
> Glory begun below.

How anyone who has caught a gleam of glory from the face of some contemporary saint can ever regard the teaching of Christ as repressive, life-denying, and tending to melancholy, is a mystery hard to explain.

From all the wrong habits of our negative thinking, from all the settled contrariness which spurns truth and perversely delights to be different, from all the fears which would make us flee from life and put up palisades of mistrust behind which to hide ourselves, he can and will deliver us.

We need his mind. His mind in our mind. Hear the vibrant voice breaking over the hillside again: "I came that you might have life and have it more abundantly."

Have this mind in you, which was also in Christ Jesus. (A.S.V.)

TO SUM UP

Some people are negative in all their thinking; their first reaction to all talk of change is "No."

Some are even militant in opposition. Whatever is suggested instantly leads them to argue for the contrary. They make perversity a "principle."

Christ was positive, life-affirming, life-bestowing.

He taught and showed that life was good and could be full, free, abounding, and happy to the point of bliss.

20

HOW MUCH DO *THINGS* MATTER?

THERE is a terrible attachment in the normal human heart and mind to *things*. The aim of life with millions of people is to get *things*. A secure position; a home, a house, a better home, a larger house; a little car, a bigger car . . . things, things, things!

In a sense, it is all natural. We live in a material world and depend in part on material things, and none but the unbalanced can be indifferent to them. Material things, at their own level, are very insistent. The most perfervid evangelist knows that you cannot preach effectively to a hungry man. You must give him a meal first and (even though it spoils the meal!) the sermon afterward. The body may not be the chief thing about any human being, but it *will* have its due. A man cannot live by bread alone but, in this world, he cannot live without it.

How much we are dependent on material things is fully known only to those who have to go without them. I remember giving a glass of milk years ago to a child in the slums, and she took a sip and looked at me, and sipped again and looked once more; and when I said, "Drink it up!" she said in an awed voice: "What! *Can I drink to the bottom?*" What years of deprivation lay behind that astonished inquiry!

A little *évacué* from East London was sent in September, 1939, to a seaside resort on the South Coast. He rose early the next morning and set out for his first glimpse of the sea. Not knowing just where it was, he asked a passer-by.

"Straight ahead!" she said. "Straight ahead!"

The little fellow hurried off again, and then a dark thought crossed his mind. He ran back to the lady who had directed him and said: *"Is it free?"*

It is behind innocent childish questions like these that we see the bitter denials of sweet and wholesome joys—joys which God meant for every child and which were withheld sometimes for want of a penny.

One cannot despise material things.

But they grow too large in the human mind. Necessary and elemental as they are, they have a way of elbowing out everything else, and people come to spend their whole lives screaming for things. They equate "life" with things. They believe that the respect of others depends largely on what we possess. They become covetous, grasping, and hoarding too.

For most people the desire for things focuses in the pursuit of money. Money commands other things. Having money, they believe, you can get everything else—comfort, enjoyment, influence, power. "Every man has his price," they say. Some have even convinced themselves that it will buy "love"!

The inability of money to satisfy the human soul has been demonstrated in every age, but people are still caught by its lure. To make the pursuit of money the main aim of life is demonstrably stupid and disappointing, but only those who get wealth know this. The mass of mankind, not having it, still believe that wealth and joy go together.

It is a stupid aim because it concerns itself with this life only. Common sense has long asserted that "You can't take it with you. There are no pockets in a shroud."

It is disappointing because, beyond a necessary but very modest level, it brings cares, griefs, and deep unease. A list of the world's wealthiest men is not a list of those enjoying the fullest life. Can anybody studying the life of J. D. Rockefeller, the multimillionaire, suppose that he was a happy man? Picture him standing before the Congressional Committee of the United States of America giving evidence at the inquiry into the ways of high finance: "The Standard Oil Company keeps no books," he said cynically.

Or read the life of J. Pierpont Morgan—the one who died in 1913—and you will be left wondering whether he was more corrupt in his business life or his private life. About one thing, however, you will not be left wondering. You will know he was not a happy man.

Or try Andrew Carnegie. Not all his public libraries and church organs can erase the stain of his steel trusts or leave one thinking that his vast wealth had brought him bliss.

Hard as some people will find it to receive, it is a fact that material things are regarded as the chief good in life only by those who do not have them. I have read enough, and talked enough with those who have succeeded in the vast accumulation of this world's goods, to be sure upon the point. They found them (sought for themselves alone) a hollow sham and incapable of meeting the deeper hunger of the heart.

Not only is the pursuit of money for its own sake folly; it is *perilous*. Material things have a way of mastering us. They deceive our poor minds with the idea that if we have *them,* we shall be masterful. In fact, they master us, and we become unconscious slaves.

There is a story of a poor man who had just enough money to support life in its simplest way and who spent his days enjoying modest pleasures and helping other people. He was once in the company of a very wealthy man who was completely immersed in business, working all the hours he was awake, and enslaved to acquisition.

"I am richer than you are," said the poor man.

"How can you say that?" the millionaire inquired.

"Well," he said, "I have as much money as I want and you haven't."

How true it is that the thing masters the life. A man made in the image of God, and with an immortal soul, lives for no other purpose than to heap together money and grows as metallic as the coin he seeks. In the end it becomes a disease. Even though the effort to get it is killing him, he cannot leave off.

I went down Cheyne Walk in Chelsea the other day, and passing No. 5, I remembered John Camden Neild. He was a miser. He inherited a quarter of a million from his father, and for thirty years he toiled and starved to double the sum. He never brushed his clothes, his shoes were down at heel, and when he visited his great estates, he lived with his poor tenants and shared their frugal meals. When he was over seventy he died and left all the money so meanly accumulated to the richest woman in the land—to Queen Victoria.

That is what money can do. It can master a man, and you do not need half a million for that to happen. Many a person who is in its grip possesses an estate beneath the interest of a serious financier. It wins when it convinces you that it is the chief thing to work for, and millions of people all over the world (and well above the subsistence level) believe that money is the chief end of man. It is the way to get *things,* and they believe that a man's life consists in the abundance of the things he possesses.

Nor is it hard to show that the domination of things extends beyond the range of the individual mind to communal and world thought. The whole world lives in the fearful shadow of a bomb. The terror of the thing fills the mind of multitudes with dread, and the hearts of men fail because of fear. Twenty airplanes each carrying a hydrogen bomb—and tens of thousands could be blasted into a swift and merciful death, and millions left to linger in agony indescribable. Nobody wants it to happen—*but things rule.*

Even the competing economic systems of the world illustrate again how things strive to master. Our standards of value today—whether capitalistic or communistic—are frankly materialistic. "They must be!" men impatiently answer. "It is a material world."

Only a material world? *Chiefly* a material world.

But the common element in both capitalism and communism is that what really matters is *things*. It is common to both that life consists in the possession and enjoyment of material goods. All their bitter quarrels with one another concern *who* shall have them, and how! Each occasionally pays lip service to higher values, but it is only lip service. Capitalism requires that food on which no profit can be made must be destroyed, though half the world is hungry and a third of it is starving. Classic communism denies any worth to man beyond the grave. He has no real *value*. Essentially he is a beast—even if a superior one. For all his large thinking and despite his claim to be the friend of the laboring man, Marx has tricked the workers of the world.

God made them a little lower than the angels. Marx would make them no better than animals. God destines them for heaven. Marx would shut them up to earth. God says, "Things are your servants, use them!" Communists and capitalists together say, by implication: "*Things* are the only things that matter. The rest is really 'pie in the sky.' "

Who can deliver us from this impasse? If only we could *see* the way it would be something. Can Christ help us here? Is it possible to perceive our errors in the mirror of his perfect life, and again from his teaching and example the help we so clearly need?

No teacher gave more solemn warning against the sin of covetousness or lived more generously than Christ. He said: "Be on your guard against covetousness in any shape or form. A man's real life does not consist in the number of things he possesses!" Then he told a story of a rich fool who hoarded and hoarded, and counted with confidence on the future years. He meant to be at ease: to eat, drink, and be merry . . . and that night he died. Anybody is a fool, said Jesus, who lays up treasure for himself and is not rich toward God.

Again and again, in varying words, the same solemn warning echoes through his teaching. "Don't pile up treasures on earth," he said, "where moth and rust can spoil them and thieves break in and steal. But keep your treasure in heaven where there is neither moth nor rust to spoil it, and nobody can break in and steal. For you may be sure your heart will be wherever you keep your treasure!"

In the Ten Commandments, covetousness is put under the ban with murder, adultery, theft, and slander. In the New Testament, covetousness and adultery are constantly classed together. It is strange that, in the long history of the Christian church, adultery should have retained its heinousness and covetousness almost disguise itself as a noble thing.

Nor did Jesus ever suggest that things as things were evil. He knew that there was a necessary minimum of material things without which life was impossible. He had a real concern about our creaturely needs. He fed the hungry, had a special tenderness toward the poor, and incited people to generosity. Indeed, during his public ministry he may have lived largely on the generosity of others himself.

He did not *scorn* things. But he knew their perilous agility in getting the mastery over the soul of man, and so he cried, "Beware of covetousness. . . . How difficult it is for those who have great possessions to get into the kingdom of God. . . . Why, a camel could more easily squeeze through the eye of a needle than a rich man get into the kingdom of God. . . . What shall it profit a man to gain the whole world and lose his own soul?"

Nor can it be doubted that those who, through the ages, have most caught the spirit of their Master have been gloriously emancipated from enslavement to things. From Jesus himself to Francis of Assisi, from Francis to John Wesley, from John Wesley to Catherine Booth, sanctity and poverty have known how to live together. None of them *despised* things. What saint can despise what God has made? But things to a saint are always his servants. Things to our world are the purpose of their toil.

And therein lies an awful peril. When things become the chief purpose of living, when money (the key to the rest of them) is seen as life's chief good, every precious thing is in danger—the integrity of the individual soul, the decency of the community, the soundness of all human life.

Professor W. E. Hocking has argued that we cannot have a sound society unless we have a sufficient number of men who cannot be bought. He called them "unpurchasable men." Religion—and supremely the religion of Christ—produces the unpurchasable man, and unpurchasable men are the salt of society. No social life is long possible unless it has its quorum of men of integrity: men whom *nothing* can buy.

The sinister, deadly character of things (and especially of money) is that they can buy a soul, bargain for and take integrity, corrupt the decencies, rot a whole community from within.

No wonder Christ pleaded with men to beware. He warned them by precept and parable of the awful consequences of this insidious enslavement, lived in poverty himself the more to illustrate that fullness of life was possible with a minimum of this world's goods, besought men ever to keep in mind as their chief treasures the values which belong to heaven.

How much do material things matter? They matter a great deal to those in acute poverty, but above that level they do not matter *very* much. They cannot be ignored and ought never to be despised. God made them and therefore they are holy in origin and ours to be enjoyed.

Enjoy them! Be truly thankful for them! Revel in the wholesome things which God has made!

But watch them. They are aiming to master your mind.

Have this mind in you, which was also in Christ Jesus. (*A.S.V.*)

TO SUM UP

There is a terrible attachment in human hearts to material things.

They can't be despised, but they grow too precious.

The desire for things focuses in the craving for money —as the key to other things.

But great wealth leaves the heart still hungry and often masters the men who think they are masters of it.

Christ lived on a minimum of material things and warned men repeatedly against covetousness.

Society will rot without men who "can't be bought," and only men who have the mind of Christ have mastered the lure of money and are truly "unpurchasable men."

21

IT'S MY BEASTLY BAD TEMPER

No consideration of the sad spiritual disorders of the human mind would be complete without a mention of bad temper. It is common in the community, quite chronic in some people, and terribly hard for other folk to live with.

People who are bad-tempered are touchy; they flare up at the least provocation (and sometimes at no provocation at all) and seem all the time to be smoldering with anger within. Their bad temper arises in some cases from the other spiritual maladies we have considered before (pride, inner unrest, resentment, or jealousy), but often its roots are in itself alone. It is just bad temper, unchecked in childhood and now built by habit into the structure of nature. Indeed, some people who are bad examples of ill temper even take pride in it as though it were a striking feature of their personality and a means of becoming known!

To live or work with the bad-tempered is a torment to the courteous and gentle. They find themselves on tenterhooks whenever the boor is around; sometimes they try to "jolly" him along and sometimes they "baby" him, but most often they submit to him. So the disease grows because it is not countered. The truth told with loving plainness would do him more good. But it would be unlikely to cure him. Bad temper shares with other sins the awful peculiarity that it blinds as it grows; the more you have of it, the less you can see; the worse you become, the more easily you accept it. In few things is it harder for a man to "get wise to himself."

It is, moreover, especially skillful in disguising itself to the conscience. Bad-tempered people always think that it is something or somebody else who is to blame for their bad temper—seldom themselves. Such a person looks upon his proneness to these outbursts as part of his make-up—like freckles or a big nose—which other people will see and must put up with because he chances to be made that way. Moral condemnation hardly enters in.

It is not without interest to go through the excuses the ill-tempered give to themselves and (occasionally) to others. Some ascribe it all to temperament, which (in this connection) only means temper too old to spank. Some put it down to their physical condition (indigestion or tiredness), from which others suffer also without making their family miserable because of it. Others, like Cassius, blame it on their parents. "My mother had a quick temper too!" Still others explain it by their race ("I'm Irish, you know!"), which can only deceive people who do not know the Irish enough to realize that they include some of the sweetest-tempered Christians one can ever meet. Some are so hard-driven that they put it down to the color of their hair! "I'm a redhead," they say (which, of course, can hardly be concealed!), but a flaming head has no connection with a flaming temper—except in the foolish superstition which has linked them together in the common mind.

And for "reasons" as paltry as these, people will hide from the truth concerning themselves, will make no resolute effort of their own will or seek help from a divine source to break a habit undignified to human nature and hurtful to other people, will go through life supposing they have an alibi for conduct which alarms people of sensibility and wounds all who have the misfortune to live with them.

It would be fair to admit, of course, that constant and unprovoked bad temper, such as we are discussing here, is not the same thing as occasional anger. Anger is natural in man. It is part of our instinctive inheritance. It is the immediate reaction of our nature to intentional injury, to militant opposition, to thwarting, and to injustice. Even so, it needs to be controlled. One mark of maturity is the ability to control anger. People who act instantly and violently at the impulse of anger go berserk. They say more than they mean, misrepresent their own better nature, give bitter expression to the darker moods of the soul, and prove themselves incapable of balanced judgment and high leadership.

The example of Jesus is sometimes cited to prove that anger is occasionally legitimate.

Of course it is! But how many can measure up to the standard of Christ?

There is no instance in the New Testament of Christ guilty of bad temper. Indeed, the mere association of his name and that sin will seem to many to border on the blasphemous. The withering of the fig tree is sometimes quoted by his opponents as an instance of petulance. But that is a superficial judgment. It would certainly be entirely out of character with everything else we learn of Christ in the Gospels. The inwardness of that incident is to be sought rather in the parabolic warning it contained to those who made much profession of religion and bore little fruit than in any failure of graciousness on the part of Christ.

Anger you will find in Christ . . . but not bad temper.

His anger, moreover, has certain striking peculiarities. He blazes with anger when most men would be quite indifferent or mildly disapproving. He is entirely free of anger when most strong men would be choked with rage.

Anger is natural at one level and supernatural at another. The natural man blazes with anger at personal injury and injustice, but bears with shocking composure the greater injuries and injustices of others. Christ bore with sublime serenity the indignities and injustices heaped upon himself and burned with anger at the foul exploitation of the truly pious and the poor. The difference is clean, clear, and enormous. Hate at its most venomous nails him to two pieces of wood and provokes him to nothing but prayers for his murderers' pardon. Nothing of anger, only prayer and love. Yet when he saw all the dirty trade in the temple courts by which hypocrites thrived on the honest devotion of the poor, he rushed on the stalls, turned them over, and whipped those grasping hucksters out of the holy place.

There is something indecent and hypocritical in anyone seeking to defend his own bad temper by talking of Christ and of "righteous indignation." The term is demeaned by such use. There is nothing blurred on the question of anger in Christ's example. We shall call anger "righteous indignation" when pure concern for the suffering of others leads a man to bold and costly action, and we shall call it something else (however natural it may be!) when their blazing indignation has been provoked by some setback to themselves. It may still seem "righteous" in their own eyes, but we are not the best judges of our own "righteousness." In any case, Christ's example is clear. Nothing that ever happened in this universe was more unrighteous than the Cross. But they did not crucify an angry man.

What can cure the chronic bad temper to which some of us are prone?—and what can control and transmute the natural anger which all of us feel?

Good advice is not enough, not even the good advice we give to ourselves. General Buller—an obdurate case of bad temper—used to give advice to himself. He was more advanced in self-knowledge than most ill-tempered people. He knew it to be the nasty sin it is, whereas most ill-tempered people (as we have seen) seem unaware of it or lightly excuse it to themselves.

But Buller knew—and one cannot withhold sympathy from a man fighting a weakness alone. Lord Esher asked him once, in confidential conversation, how he had put himself in a position to be hopelessly misunderstood and never again trusted by his countrymen. Buller said:

> It is my beastly temper. All my life long I have suffered from this. Since old Eton days I have had a formula for myself: "Remember Dunmore." It happened in this way. At a football match, the ball came to me and I had it in my power to run down and secure a goal; but I stopped to have a "shinning match" with Dunmore and lost my chance. Although always present in my mind, I have always failed to remember Dunmore.

Good advice is not enough. He said it was "present to his mind" but he "always failed to remember." He must have meant that the mental recollection produced no influence on the will. He had started on the way to recovery because he was "wise to himself" and knew the peril, yet he failed.

What *can* help us to see ourselves as we are, and see ourselves as we might be?

Nothing so much as gazing in the mirror of Christ! There we shall see the truth as it is, and there we shall see the hope of the future.

Look again into the garden of Gethsemane. The vigil and the struggle are over, and the Son of man is ready for betrayal, trial, and death. Noises are heard, a lantern gleams in the darkness, and a group of men armed with swords and cudgels advance on that bloodstained Man. Judas Iscariot is leading them. He comes up to Jesus and kisses him. Was ever a symbol of love more foully misused?

But Jesus does not spurn him, nor is there a hint of cynicism in his use of a word which—without being the word he usually employed—

can still be translated, "Friend!" "Friend," he says, "do what you've come for."

If injustice (as many people believe) is the hardest thing to bear, and if deep disloyalty is loathsome to the point of nausea, what an occasion for indignation! And who could deny that it would have been "righteous"? But there is no indignation. Dignity marks all his bearing and love fills his heart.

Almost in the instant that Judas kissed him, the soldiers closed in on Christ. Peter pulled out his concealed sword and aimed at the nearest. He meant it for his head but it only got his ear. Nor was the victim a soldier. It turned out to be Malchus, a servant of the high priest; but if Jesus spoke sharply, it was not to Malchus (though he had come to help in the arrest), but to the baffled and bewildered Peter. "Put your sword back into its place" (R.S.V.), he said to Peter. To Malchus he turned and touched him to healing. So the last cure of his incarnate life was worked on one who had come to drag him to death. So at the end as at the beginning, love and hate met in deadly battle . . . and love won.

All that followed ran to the same pattern. Lies, insults, brutalities, and a torturing death—but no anger in him. He who had called those highly placed hypocrites "whited sepulchres" to their face, he who had flamed out against the "holy" men who allowed commerce in the temple courts and got their "rake-off" from it, he who displayed on occasion the terrible "anger of the Lamb" at injustices done to others . . . how meekly he suffers the indignities and injuries heaped on himself!

What amazing serenity! What unearthly self-mastery! What utter nobility of mind!

Have this mind in you, which was also in Christ Jesus. (*A.S.V.*)

TO SUM UP

Bad temper is a common fault.

It is sometimes a consequence of other maladies in the mind and sometimes it is simply *bad temper*.

People who are guilty of it dodge any shame on the point by shallow excuses and by blaming other people for provoking it in them. "*You* made me bad-tempered!"

Occasional anger is natural and justifiable. Christ was angry now and then.

A careful study of the character of his anger clears up all our difficulties of understanding on the point and makes us long again for "the mind that was in Christ."

22

I HAVE A BATTLE WITH EVIL THOUGHTS

We cannot conclude our study of the major maladies which afflict the mind of man without considering the long battle which many people have with lewd desire. In some natures all other troubles are minor in comparison with this.

"But is sexual lust," someone might ask, "strictly speaking, a matter of the mind at all? Does it not rather belong to the *body?* Is not that side of our nature fairly described in the Bible and elsewhere as being of the 'flesh'?"

No sharp distinction can be drawn between mind and body. The mind does not live within the body as a kernel exists within the shell of a nut. Mind and body are interwoven in a way not yet fully understood, but each acts and reacts upon the other.

And yet certain desires can truly be said to belong to the body—sexual desires. They are divine in origin and come to us as powerful instincts. If they were to cease to function, it would mean that our race would vanish from the earth.

It is prudish to be ashamed of them. One might as well be ashamed of hunger. God made us that way, and to call anything which God has made "common" or "unclean" is to be guilty of profanity. God did few things more wonderful with his earth-born creatures than when he half lifted them from their creaturely status and shared with them the joy of creation. Be glad to be normal. Those people who are secretly ashamed of the normal appetites of nature are unconsciously finding fault with the God who made them.

But all that only proves how great is the battle some people fight in their minds. In giving us life inter-penetrated by great instincts—self, sex, the herd—God never said (as sinful men have tried to argue in all generations) that every instinct brings its own immediate justification with it, that to want a thing is reason enough for taking it, that morals are only social conventions to be scorned at the impulse of strong desire. Life comes to us with powerful instinctive urges, but God has said that we must not weakly yield ourselves to the varying stresses of instinct, but rather build a life in which morals shall regulate appetite and spiritual purposes shall guide the passions of the flesh.

Hence, though self is so strongly assertive within us, we have seen how self-centeredness must die; and we see also that though the advantage of our own group is most demanding in our nature, real progress requires concern for other groups also and ultimately for all the human race. Though the mating instinct is built into our very nature, we recognize that it must be entirely denied to some people, fully surrendered by others, and sternly disciplined in all. Therein lies the battle, and the battle is not chiefly in the body but chiefly *in the mind*.

Indeed, we can almost indicate the "areas" of the mind which are most involved. The *imagination* is the scene of much of the fighting. A thought comes to the mind, and no man or woman need be ashamed of that. It is rooted in nature. A picture, a word, a story, an advertisement, a glance, an odor . . . almost anything could summon the thought to the mind, and in a passionate nature it is soon hot with desire. Victory or defeat turns on the skill and the speed with which that thought is managed in the mind. If a man turns his thought swiftly to cooler things, if (being a Christian) he thinks on Christ and turns to prayer, if (knowing his own nature and the need for nimble wits) he keeps in the antechamber of his mind certain engrossing and wholesome themes to which he can turn his thought at any time by a simple act of will, those appetites of the flesh can be kept in place. Temptation is not sin. The firm routine of disciplined thinking will save his vagrant thoughts from mounting into lust and he will have a well-knit character.

But if, on the other hand, he toys with the thought, if he allows his eager imagination to indulge itself, if he fingers the idea and holds up pictures on the walls of his fancy, if he wallows in absorbing daydreams of things that should not be and gluts his mind in visions he should have blasted with a prayer, all his lusts will be inflamed and the animal will triumph in him. Anything can happen to such a man. Having lost the battle in his mind and imagination, the defeat works itself out in the flesh. He can become a pervert. He can walk about with dirty postcards in his pocket and tell himself that he is interested in "art." He can develop a greedy appetite for pornographic literature, from the worst kind of Sunday newspaper to the type of book which it is still (thank God!) an offense to publish in many countries. He can be a vendor of smutty stories. He may think that he is still master of his mind and could break free at any time, but he is self-deceived and someday he will know it. He lost the battle in his imagination, and his mind (as Montaigne said) has become "a merry-go-round of lustful images."

The disproportion of the sexes (especially after costly wars) consigns thousands of good women made for motherhood to the unmated life. Economic circumstances compel celibacy in many young men through what can be most testing years. A proper continence is required of Christians within the marriage bond. We do not need to take the pulse of our nation on this subject to realize its importance and peril. We need only reflect on our own nature. Yet it is a fact that the nation is in no small danger by the wide abandonment of thousands of people to animal lust. The Chairman of the Association of British Travel Agents said a while ago that visitors to this country constantly expressed horror at the shamelessness of this immoral traffic in London. Soliciting on the streets of our capital city is open and blatant. It is considered by many widely traveled people to be without parallel in the Western world. What need there is for moral revival in the life of our nation! What need there is for moral strengthening in our individual lives as well!

The standard of Christ in all that makes for sexual purity has seemed to many people impossibly high. Morals had an inwardness for him which made the intention of the soul the subject of the ethical judgment and not alone the deed. He said: "Every one that looks on a woman to lust after her has committed adultery with her already in his heart."

His meaning in that statement must be carefully balanced to avoid distortion either way. Christ is not equating temptation with sin. Sexual desire welling up from any man's carnal nature is not sin. It is, at that stage, normal instinct bidding for moral stature. Nor does it need to wait until it solidifies in an act to become sin. It becomes sin when the self welcomes it, adopts it, owns it, nurtures it . . . . Then, said Christ, that lusting man has committed adultery already. His inability or fearfulness to turn the will into a deed is irrelevant to the morality. He is guilty in identifying himself with the desire. It all happens in the mind and will. On Christ's view of morality, a man could keep the Ten Commandments and be a moral leper too.

The example of Jesus in this, as in everything else, bears out his teaching. He was born among a people who took a low view of woman. A Jew would not greet a woman on the street, much less talk with her there. In morning prayer, a Jew blessed God that he was not made a gentile, a slave, or a *woman*. It was impious for a Jew to teach a woman the law.

Yet in all the contacts recorded in the Gospels between Christ and women there is nothing in him which is not respectful and indeed sympathetic. His attitude toward them has altered the whole attitude of the Western world.

He talked to them—and not *down* to them. He had close friends among them. The Bible says that he loved Martha and Mary. Penitent harlots were in his own inner circle.

Moreover, his purity was so white and burning that it did not need to be guarded. Carnal sin in his presence flared into self-consciousness and grew deeply ashamed.

Picture him by the well at Sychar. Being tired, Jesus sat by the well, and his friends went away to buy food. When they returned, they "marveled."

They might well do. They had three grounds for marveling. He was talking to a *woman* who was a *Samaritan* and a *harlot*. The woman was staggered herself when he addressed her.

That was the kind of thing which Jesus did naturally. Salvation was from the Jews, but it was for all. In him there was neither male nor female. As for her sin, it could not even challenge the burning purity of Christ. Even when he wore our flesh our God was "a consuming fire."

Or see him at the Temple when they bring before him the woman taken in adultery. It was a trap, and a peculiarly clever one. Whatever he said, they had him. If he said, "Stone her," he could be accused of encroaching on the rights of the Romans, who alone had the authority of life and death. If he said, out of his well-known tenderness to sinners, "Let her go," then he was contravening the law of Moses, which made death the penalty for adultery.

He said neither. He said: "Let the one without sin among you cast the first stone" . . . and one by one they slunk off.

Perhaps only Jesus could have said that . . . and achieved the effect he did. Such words to be powerful could only be uttered beneath the sounding board of a life of awesome purity. It is an oblique testimony to the white heat of his holiness.

To the woman he said: "Neither do I condemn thee. Go, and sin no more."

No wonder this little fragment of Gospel narrative found it hard to secure a firm place in the Bible. It *must* have happened. It has all the stamp of the Master upon it . . . and yet we do not find it hard to understand why so many of the early scribes left it out. How lax and dangerous it seems! *"Neither do I condemn thee!"* . . . from the One "of purer eyes than to behold iniquity."

But those early copyists need not have been so timid for their God. It was *because* he was so pure that he could be so kind. Why would sinful men fear to say such a thing?—or fear to set the saying down as from the lips of Christ?

The guilt inside a sinner would cry out against it. His past wrongdoing, his little bit of hard-won goodness, and his honest sternness with himself would tremble that so grave a breach of morals should pass without a word of condemnation. But there was no guilt in Jesus to make his forgiveness self-excusing. His purity speaks his pardon. Only the holy God could acquit like that; only holiness can excuse a sinner without at the same time excusing oneself. It is God's prerogative to forgive or condemn, and it is the holy God who says: "Neither do I condemn thee. Go, and sin no more."

If tempted men and women are to find the strength to resist the fierce impulses built into the very structure of their lives, it is from Christ that they must get it. He lifts the standard to unbelievable heights, but he imparts the power to reach it. He carries the moral tests into the deep recess of the soul, but he gives the grace to pass them. It is the claim of all who know Christ with intimacy that he is able to meet men and women in the awful moral predicament in which they find themselves . . . and save them.

He is skillful in all the three necessary steps.

He shows us in himself the men we might be. He holds up the living example of what human nature could be for men and women alike.

He shows us the persons we now are. Most people (as we have seen) are quite ignorant of themselves. "Getting wise to oneself" turns out to be a far more difficult task than we had supposed. Introspection (conducted on one's own) is hard, can be sadly self-deceiving, and in some natures is even morbid and dangerous. Introspection (conducted with Christ) is painful, but it is honest and can be completely healing. It is not flattering to human nature to discover how selfish and proud we can be, or fearful and inferior, or resentful and jealous. It is humbling to the point of abasement to realize that we are guilty of self-pity and a bundle of negatives, or essentially materialistic at heart, or bad-tempered and secretly lustful. But whatever we are (and these major maladies by no means exhaust all the disorders of the soul), Christ can show them embedded in our own nature and *yet not spurn us.* He does not leave us hopeless in self-loathing and despair. He shows us what we are. He shows us what we could be, *and he puts the ladder in between.*

It is that ladder we must now climb.

We need, with his help, to mount to another plane of thinking. More than we realized, our life is our thought. "As a man thinks . . . so is he." We have found sickness and sin in our minds, but the offer of the New Testament is that our minds can be transformed. We murmur the challenging words again and savor the promise at their heart.

Be ye transformed by the renewing of your mind.

Have this mind in you, which was also in Christ Jesus. (*A.S.V.*)

Be renewed in the spirit of your mind.

All we need now to know is *how*. We are convinced of the need and convinced of the possibility. We accept the divine imperative:

Have this mind in you, which was also in Christ Jesus. (*A.S.V.*)

TO SUM UP

The great engrossment of the mind of many people is lust; they burn with sexual passion.

The instinct is divine in origin and at the heart of many lovely things; but grown greedy with undisciplined indulgence, it becomes sheer carnality.

It does not belong only to the flesh (as some think), but ensnares us in the imagination. The battle is in the mind.

The purity of Christ shone and burned.

His attitude toward women has transformed the whole attitude of the Western world.

He lends his strength to tempted men and women, and by his help they also can be pure.

PART THREE

THE WAY

The Path Between

23

HOW TO BEGIN

We begin the constructive part of our thinking by repeating certain great convictions:

That God is on the throne and God is love.

That God was revealed in Christ—as completely as ever Deity can be revealed within humanity.

That God in Christ will come and dwell in all human hearts that are consecrated to him and who sincerely desire the divine indwelling. For the purposes of our thinking here, we need make no distinction among the indwelling of Father, Son, or Holy Spirit. The very nature of the Holy Trinity assures us that we have the Three in One and One in Three. If we have focused our quest as the quest for the mind of Christ, we do so because the Bible so instructs us, and because it is in Jesus that the great triune God comes nearest to our understanding. The consecration of our lives to him is an essential prerequisite of the divine indwelling.

But (oddly enough, in some ways) personal consecration is not enough. When we raised the question why some Christians are not radiant (taking radiance as the outward shine of the divine indwelling) we could not accuse them of hypocrisy. We were forced to conclude of the majority of them that they had honestly declared their allegiance to Christ without understanding his offer to control their minds; they had run up his flag, as it were, on the keep of their castle, but it had not made much difference to what was going on inside. In the minds of multitudes of people who sincerely regard themselves as Christian, the old muddled, soiled, and fearful thinking goes on; traffic still runs on the old habit tracks, and they have an "underworld" life on which their professed allegiance to Christ seems to have no effect at all.

We repeat that this is seldom conscious hypocrisy. People do not know themselves. Getting wise to oneself turns out to be more difficult and more painful than we had supposed. Indeed, it seems plainly impossible undertaken alone. Hence the discipline of looking into the mirror of Christ, where we can see in one steady gaze both the men we are and the men we can be. Hence, also, the conclusion which we are forced to draw that though we have sincerely professed allegiance to Christ and sought to follow him, we have not been transformed by the renewing of our mind.

How, then, can we put ourselves in the way of this transformation? How can we have the mind that was in Christ?

Clearly we cannot have it without wanting it, but wanting it is not enough.

Few people brought to see themselves in Christ would still *not* want it. Love for hate? Gladness for sorrow? Peace for inner unrest? Freedom from paralyzing fear and inferiority? Victory over envy, resentment, self-pity, and lust? Only the perverse would not *want* it . . . and if we do not want it enough, the experience of it will make us want it more, and God can be trusted to warm the desire for himself in any mind and heart where he is welcome.

But even when we want it, we can still wonder *how* it can be. How does one mind—even the divine mind—come into another? Surely not by one stroke of omnipotence on God's part, or one act of will on ours. God does not deal with us by strokes of omnipotence. He respects the personalities which he has made. He *must* do so. Virtue is the fine fruit of freedom and it is virtue he wants. If he took from us our freedom, he could have a perfect world of machines immediately—with every robot doing just what the divine Engineer desired. But wanting a world of good *men and women*, he stands at the door and knocks. He will not *impose* his mind on ours. If we are to have the mind that was in Christ, it can come only by our willingness, our free co-operation, our eager readiness to have it so.

And if one stroke of omnipotence on God's part must be ruled out as impossible and ineffective, so must one act of will on ours. By one act of will, as we have seen, a man may declare his allegiance to Christ; by one act of will, he may run up Christ's flag on the castle of his life . . . but not by one act of will can he receive Christ's mind.

One act of will may register his readiness for a life of discipline in the school of Christ. That single act of will would be very important. One resolute act of will (and God's help) could put us under the tutelage of the Holy Spirit, and if we stayed there, what an important and revolutionizing act that would be! But the simple truth is that to have the mind of Christ *we must give him our mind,* and that is a matter of the firmest daily discipline. It will involve us in mental-spiritual exercises to which no one who honestly aspires after the prize can ever feel superior. It will take time and patience and resolution and daily work . . . and those who are unready for it had better abandon the enterprise at once. To give somebody a shilling is simple. A moment of time and a move of the hand and it is done. But to give someone your mind is a vastly different thing.

When a person in perplexity turns for help to a minister of religion, a minister who knows his business gives the troubled soul his whole mind. He listens to the story completely absorbed. If he interrupts at all, it is only for a moment and in order that he may more fully understand. When the story is told, he goes over it again so that every fact has its place and every nuance in the voice of his visitor has been interpreted. He seeks to identify himself with the person before him; he thinks his thoughts, feels with him in the changing emotions of the unfolding story, and seems almost to slip into their skin and live their life within them.

Meanwhile, his mind is open to God. He is aware (at the *same* time) of being open upward and outward. His experience of life and of counseling people never betrays him into supposing that he can settle this problem by himself. He remembers the uniqueness of every soul. He remembers that some of the story may not have been told; some part forgotten and some part too painful to tell. He remembers his own frailty. But he listens two ways. To the troubled soul—and to God; and in that concentration, and more by God than by his own judgment, he often finds the answer that is sought. He is prompted to ask a question, perhaps, the full import of which he himself does not see in asking it. Or he probes into something seemingly irrelevant and the whole thing breaks open. A shaft of light explodes the dark heart of the problem, and his visitor departs knowing what to do and inwardly assured that it is right.

The answer does not always come in one interview. Often the minister must see the person again and again and go to God himself in private for the illumination that he needs, but this simple picture lifted from the day-to-day life of a minister of God will put richer meaning into the repetitive phrase: "I gave him my whole mind." The concentration of thought; the inward self-identification; the living in the life of another; thinking, feeling, and willing, as it were, in the soul of someone else . . . what a costly thing it is in some ways, and yet (undertaken with God) how rewarding too!

In some such way as this (and with the roles, of course, reversed) we have to give our minds to Christ. Daily waiting on him. Increasing concentration of thought. Learning how to outwit our tendency to mind-wandering. Schooling ourselves to wait while the clamorous world drops away. Recognizing the place and times of closest contact. Holding to the moments of closest communion when "time and sense seem all no more." Drawing into ourselves by the suction of longing the very life of God which can transform our souls.

It will seem to some theologically-minded people that this is more like *work* than God's way of salvation was meant to be. All the fullness of God, they will argue, is available to anyone who will "only believe."

And how true that is in some ways! If "believing" meant that utter trust in Christ and love of him which would lead them to keep with unfailing faithfulness their daily tryst and draw into their souls the life of God himself, it would be enough to say "only believe."

But many who talk about "only believing" mean accepting a formula, subscribing to a set of words, assenting to certain formal propositions or creedal tests. Their believing has not drawn the life of God into their souls. They are grim, they are fearful, they are envious, they are proud. Love does not burn in them, joy does not well from them, peace does not shine through them.

The life of Christ is not to be had cheaply. It cost him a Cross, and it will cost us more than the repetition of a formula. To those with theological interests it will be enough to say that the discipline of mind here advocated has nothing to do with "working one's passage to heaven." It is not "salvation by works" coming in at the back door. It is, on the contrary, the very effort to give salvation by faith reality and richness. The discipline advocated here is not one of service which will build up the merit of good work—later to be crowned by God with salvation—but the discipline of devotion which will so open our nature to him that he can answer our own longing:

Heavenly Adam, Life Divine,
Change my nature into Thine.

And from a nature so changed better works will flow than unchanged nature could ever achieve. The discipline is all a discipline of receiving, not of doing. The doing follows inevitably from that nature so remade, and all the deeds are the deeds of Christ.

Yet the discipline is there. Wrong habits of thinking and feeling are not broken in a moment or broken in a month. Indeed, as we saw when we considered the mystery of church officials who repel us, it is easily possible for a ship to change its flag but keep its course. The man does not commit gross and vulgar sins (perhaps never committed them), but his thoughts have not changed their channels. He may still be a materialist at heart (Doesn't that deacon drive a hard bargain?), or a whiner, or chronically self-centered, or rigid in self-righteousness.

No man is changed till his mind is changed. We do most of our living within. Our deeds express our thoughts. It is into our minds that Christ must come if he is to come into our lives. From our minds, he will shape our character, discipline our will, and control our bodies. The name of Christ on our lips and the profession of Christ in our lives is not enough. "Christ in us" is the promise and "Christ in us" is our faith. "A Christ not *in* us is a Christ not ours."

Have we faith for this thing?

The New Testament gives us a picture of the world surrounded by the power of God seeking to break through. It breaks through at the point of faith. A little faith and a little breaks through, more faith and more breaks through, much faith and it comes in as a flood.

It is the largeness of their faith which makes the saints the wonderful men and women that they are. By their faith Christ comes into them and transforms their minds and often works wonders in their world. Think of the surging power of God waiting to burst into your life and to scour out all the evil sediment. "Resentments, inferiorities, bad temper . . . it can all go," said Christ, "according to your faith!"

Have you faith for a permanent change of mind? Do you believe that he could make you anew?

Handley Moule said:

Lord and Saviour, true and kind,
Be the master of my mind.[1]

He gave primacy to the primal thing. It is the mind which rules. With the imagination—so strong a segment of the mind—it shapes the will. Even when we think the flesh is ruling, it is because the mind has coaxed the carnal appetites and permitted it. *"As a man thinks,"* says the Bible, *"so is he."*

No wonder, then, that Paul insisted: "Have this mind in you, which was also in Christ Jesus." From the mind of Christ, all good things will flow. Good conduct. Good relations. High service.

We have to learn, then, how to receive the mind of Christ. It will not be easy. Without the promised help of God, we might well despair. Not easily are the thought-forms of half a lifetime broken. Not easily are the biased inheritances of our race and family recast.

But we put nothing beyond the power of grace and gladly put ourselves in school to Christ. When the Bible says: "He will keep them in perfect peace whose minds are stayed on him," we know at once that the operative word is the word "stayed." Our minds are not easily stayed on anything, least of all on the best things. Few of us are willing to keep a firm half hour early in the day for God. When we make the time and seek to stay our minds on him, our thoughts dart off in a dozen different directions. Humdrum duties pluck at our sleeve. Pleasures pull us away. The first returns seem so small that, having spent most of the time dragging our mind back from its wanderings, we are tempted to believe that we are throwing our moments away! It is so easy to give up.

Yet nothing is more rewarding. What is it worth to you to build a barrier against nervous disorders; to keep yourself wide open to the stream of God's health; to receive into your life, love, joy, peace, power, wisdom, beauty, freedom, grace . . . ? All are yours! God said so. They are waiting to come in. They are components of the mind of Christ. You cannot make them, force them, or find them. You need only *let* them.

"Let the peace of Christ rule in your hearts," said Paul. (A.S.V., R.S.V.)

[1] "Lord and Saviour, True and Kind." Used by permission of the trustees of the author's estate.

Have *faith* for it!—and to have faith for things is to believe *now* that you already have them. God is eager to give you all these things. Of that there is no shadow of doubt. Have faith for them therefore. Affirm your possession as a mark of your faith.

Begin with this simple meditation which will open your life to all the fullness of God.

Meditation I

There are nine major marks of God's presence in a human life:

LOVE, JOY, PEACE, PATIENCE, KINDNESS,
GOODNESS, FAITHFULNESS, HUMILITY,
SELF-CONTROL.

Get alone if you can.
Let all sense of strain and breathlessness go.
Be quiet in the presence of God.
Say slowly to yourself:

"In Christ, I am filled with *love,*"
"In Christ, I am filled with *joy,*"
"In Christ, I am filled with *peace,*"
etc.

Make the affirmation aloud.
Let it be loud enough to fall quietly on your ear.
Pause after each affirmation and dwell on the final word.
Think it. Feel it. Feel it *fill* you.
Each in turn, claim each grace.
Claim it ***in Christ.*** It is false outside him.

"In Christ, I am filled with *patience,*"
"In Christ, I am filled with *kindness,*"
etc.

As you come to each final word, hold it in your warm believing heart.

The meditation can be done *mentally* in a train or as you wait for a bus.

Faith fixed on these aspects of Christ's mind brings these aspects of Christ's mind into yours.

The transforming process has begun.

24

HOW TO BEGIN CLEAN

Nobody comes to Christ clean. All commerce with heaven begins (on the human side) with penitence. There was an idea abroad in the church a generation ago that young people growing up in Christian homes and in church life did not need forgiveness. They had no sins to forgive! Almost everybody in the church believed it—except the honest young people themselves. They knew they had sins. Their earliest memories included battles with their own wayward natures and while temptation is not sin, they knew that in those battles they had not always won the victory. Confronted with Christ, they knew also that they did not need only a hero. They needed cleansing too.

Everybody confronted with Christ knows that he needs cleansing. The painful discipline of gazing steadily into the mirror of his perfect life has that inevitable consequence. Undertaken with seriousness, it reveals even to the smug the selfishness and pride in our nature, the resentment, jealousy, and latent lust as well.

How does one find purity? How is it possible to begin again clean?

The Greeks had a word for purgation. They called it "catharsis." It was meant to imply a radical cleansing, the discharge of all impurities.

Nor has the word remained only medical in its use. Aristotle carried it over to the realm of the mind and heart. He used it to describe the outlet for emotion provided by drama—a means whereby the pent-up feelings within could burst out and run away.

Almost everybody knows this longing for a vent—both of the impurities of our life and of the overcharged emotions of the heart. Often the impurities and the emotions are bound up with one another. We recognize something we have done as a sin, and an awful tide of remorse rolls over us. Our hearts are nigh to bursting, but we are powerless to alter the past.

Tears are a kind of catharsis. Women often say that they "feel better after a good cry." The emotion has eased itself by this expression and half run away in tears.

But women cry more easily than men. There is something very moving in the tears of a man. Stand behind Peter outside the court of the high priest when, after cursing and swearing, he has denied that he ever knew Christ. He weeps bitterly. He shakes with sobs. The dreadful deed of which he was a spectator; the deep disloyalty of which he had been guilty; the dirty language he had dropped since knowing Jesus, but which had rushed from his mouth in the panic of the moment and fallen with incredibility even on his own startled ear . . . it all came over him as a flood. He had come to think of himself almost as a national figure, and now he knew he was just a vulgar, blaspheming fisherman after all.

And that look which Jesus gave him! In all the wicked mummery of the examination in the high priest's palace, it was not of himself that the Savior was thinking, but still of others. And (in that moment) he was thinking especially of Peter! Only Peter could have known what those eyes were saying to him. With the crowing of the cock still hanging on the air, Christ said in a look: "I warned you, Peter, yet . . . *I'm loving you still!"* It must have been that. Christ's tender, wounded look unsealed that fount of tears. Tears alone do not save us. They are a minor catharsis, but not a cure. The tears did not save Peter. He had to meet his risen Lord and be restored by Jesus—as all men must.

If tears cannot save, what can?

Christ can! He can meet us at every point of our need and save us. Being God, he can forgive sins. Knowing the longing of a truly penitent heart to make amends (even though of ourselves we can never wash away our sin), he will guide us in restitution. Restitution, when it is possible, is a mark of our penitence. The scoundrel who robbed a poor widow, claimed to have got forgiven by God, and then rattled the money in his pocket under the widow's window, was a humbug through and through.

But restitution is not always possible and *never* wipes out the sin. The grave part of sin is not against our neighbor, but against God. Only God can completely forgive. Yet Christ comes assuring us of that forgiveness and placarding the way of it on a stark cross before our eyes.

God in Christ is *all* forgiving,
Waits His promise to fulfil.

The trouble with many people who go to God for forgiveness—and even claim to have received it!—is that they cannot forgive themselves. The forgiveness seems never to have penetrated into their minds. Or they regard selfishness, fear, and inferiority as being weaknesses rather than sin—something that God either cannot or will not do anything about. Envy, self-pity, and bad temper often come into the same category in their thought. So they live; professing to be forgiven and empowered; but with this litter of worry, inferiority, and negativism matted together inside them; and getting the religion they embraced a bad name. The worldly look at them and laugh: "If that is all religion can do for that poor worried worm, I cannot be missing very much in passing it by."

The fact is that many who claim to be forgiven are still carrying their sins. Forgiveness is only a legal term with them. It has not become a spiritual fact. The burden has not rolled from them as it did from Christian in *Pilgrim's Progress* when he came to the cross. They do not feel the freedom and release of inner cleansing. Their natures are not penetrated by trust and confidence. They need to realize and complete the catharsis Christ provides, and the victory must be won again in the mind. To say with the lips, "I am forgiven. I am made anew in Christ. I have a loving Father watching over me, and all things work together for good in my life," . . . and then go about with a hangdog look, whining, fearful, deeply dissatisfied, and nursing resentments toward others, is to make it plain that no great purgation ever took place . . . or else that the cleansed heart has filled up again with all uncleanness.

How can a man deal with this recurrent problem? Is there a daily draining of the daily defilement? Can one begin each clean, new morning, clean inside?

It is a bad thing for any forgiven man or woman to dwell in his mind on his sins. It is a bad thing for any man or woman to understand by the word "sin" only the gross and vulgar sins for which the police could lock one up. We have wasted our time looking in the mirror of Christ if we have not recognized selfishness, pride, fear, envy, self-pity, resentment, and negativism as sins also.

God has forgiven us our past sins, and it is not his will that these evil things should dwell in us in future. Faith believes in their banishment. Faith steps forward and grasps by anticipation the thing which is to be.

From all iniquity, from *all,*
He shall my soul redeem;
In Jesus I believe, and shall
Believe myself to Him.

Believe for the banishment of unhealthy fear, distrust, inferiority, envy, bad temper, pride, and selfishness. *Believe* for it. See yourself without them. See yourself without them *by dwelling on the opposite.* Let confidence banish fear, humility banish pride, quiet dignity take the place of inferiority, and good will usurp the place of all resentment. *See* the coveted grace already victorious within you.

Send faith before to grasp it
Till faith be lost in sight.

Having recognized your sin, repented of it, and got forgiven, have no more truck with it. Let it go!

Being the kind of creatures we are, with strong instinctive urges in various directions, strange things can well out of our subconsciousness. That ought not to appall us in itself. In part of our nature we are related to the beasts. Those instinctive urges have had important parts to play at earlier stages in the long history of our race and have important parts to play still under the discipline of Christ.

But appetite and temptation are not sins. I need not go into a monastery because I discover that I am a man. If I do, it is still *as a man* that I go! Nature capering inside me is no more a moral fact at that stage than the bubbling steel is moral which could make either the shell of a hydrogen bomb or a set of surgical instruments. I am not ashamed to be human since God has made me so. But I will so receive by faith the mind of Christ that my better nature will run to the mold his perfect mind desires and the rest can drain away as metal mixed with impurities drains off in the molding shed.

Some people seek to clear their minds of worry and fear, fret and envy, self-pity and ill temper, by a picture of impurities flowing away. It will serve as a useful mental device in those times when our old enemies suddenly flare up and almost bring us to panic. Even then it is normally better to turn the mind resolutely to their opposites. Exclude them by dwelling on the grace which shuts them out.

But when these mental maladies seem to seize the mind for a while, the picture of the disappearing waste may have a minor use also. See these undesirable things in your imagination, filtering away, or loaded on a sludge vessel and being dropped in the depth of the sea.

Do you know what a sludge vessel is? Sludge vessels are a most important part of the sanitary system of London. When millions of people congregate together in one city, it takes little imagination to realize that the maintenance of their health is a vast problem. Most people give little thought to sewers, but only a thorough and hygienic sewage system can secure any large city from epidemics and make certain that waste and refuse will be disposed of with such speed and disinfectant firmness that disease is not given a chance. The sewage system of London is said to be one of the wonders of the sanitary world.

Not all sewage is waste. Some part is made into organic manure. A small quantity is treated to produce a fuel gas. But when every use has been made of the city's refuse, there remains an irreducible and dangerous sediment called sludge. What can be done with the sludge?

London has four sludge vessels. They are tankers really, with a cargo-carrying capacity of 1,500 tons. On every weekday tide, two of the sludge vessels set out laden with this unwanted and perilous matter and travel down the Thames to Black Deep, a depression on the bed of the ocean, fifteen miles off Foulness. When the vessel reaches Black Deep, the valves are opened and the complete cargo runs out in about twenty minutes. Down it goes, down into the salt aseptic sea. A dark stain spreads over the wake of the ship; but so wide is the ocean, and so deep the declivity, and so briny the sea that within one hour samples of water taken either from the surface of the sea or the bed of the estuary prove to be completely innocuous. The sludge has gone, devitalized of all evil power and never to be seen again. It has sunk from all human ken in the cavernous hollow of Black Deep, and has lost its evil nature on the way. So the city's health is guarded!

John Wesley knew a deeper hollow than Black Deep. He knew what he called a "bottomless abyss." He knew a medium more powerful to deal with evil than even the deep salt sea. It was the love of God made manifest in the flowing blood of Christ. Once he turned a German hymn into English, and the third verse runs like this:

> O Love, Thou bottomless abyss,
>   My sins are swallowed up in Thee!
> Covered is my unrighteousness,
>   Nor spot of guilt remains on me,
> While Jesu's blood through earth and skies
> Mercy, free, boundless mercy! cries.

That is the place for sin—the *only* place. Drop it in that bottomless abyss. There is nowhere else in the wide world where, being put, it will not remain active as evil. Only there can the sinful principle be broken, and only there has it really "gone."

Some people (as we noticed in Chapter 7) go to God for forgiveness and profess to believe that they have it—yet seem never able to forgive themselves. They walk in shadows all their days because of something which God has pardoned and pledged himself to remember no more.

But *they* remember it!—and not only rarely (when a chance remark might unavoidably bring it to mind), but regularly and with emotional turmoil, and of set purpose. They dwell on it, and seem to torture themselves with memory. They almost make the forgiveness of God of no effect. Certainly the pardon of the Almighty has failed to bring joy to their melancholy hearts.

It would shock them to suggest it, but they seem almost to imply that God's word is not to be trusted. If they protest that they *do* believe in God's forgiveness even if they cannot forgive themselves, they are unconsciously claiming to be more tender in conscience than the holy God himself. If God takes a "light" view of sin, they can't! The unconscious blasphemy of it!

God has forgiven you. Let no one accuse you—not even yourself! Whenever that lying accusation rises in your soul, murmur aloud: "No spot of guilt remains on me." Who are you to make the blood of Christ of no effect? How dare you suggest that the God who suffered crucifixion for sin is too "easy" on a moral point? How comes it that when Christ would drop that deed of yours into the bottomless abyss you must snatch it from his pierced hand and keep it quivering in your unforgiving heart.

God has forgiven you! Forgive yourself!

Start again! Start clean!

Meditation II

Picture yourself standing on the end of Southend Pier. It thrusts itself out for more than a mile into the estuary of the Thames. Clean, strong, health-giving breezes are blowing around you. A vessel in mid-channel plows on to the open sea. It is a sludge vessel, doing its important part in keeping the city of London clean.

> (Some people are so "nice" that they do not like to think of these things.
>
> They are "overnice." Nor are they improved by prudery.
>
> Sin is not nice. But we all have it.)

As the stout little vessel plows on, load it, in imagination, with your sin.

Mentally place aboard all that God has forgiven—but which you find so hard to forgive yourself.

The little ship is going to Black Deep, and when the cargo is gone, it is gone for good.

Put your worries aboard too. Toss on your pride. Bundle your resentments together; they can go as well. Make a heap of all the soiled unsavory things you found when looking into the mirror of Christ. Picture yourself loading the ship with the lot.

There it goes! It is on the way to Black Deep. It is going for ever and ever . . . .

And now recall that all your forgiven sins go into a deeper declivity than Black Deep.

Murmur the verse beginning:

> O Love, Thou bottomless abyss,
> My sins are swallowed up in Thee!

25

HOW TO COVET

Jesus once said, "Beware of covetousness," and some people have supposed that covetousness is always, and in all circumstances, wrong.

They are mistaken. A close study of the teaching of Christ would leave them in no doubt that covetousness is only wrong when it is directed to a wrong end. Directed to a right end it is the wisest, soundest, most rewarding attitude of mind and heart that any man and woman could entertain.

Paul said, "Covet earnestly the best gifts," and Christ would have said no less. To learn to covet the best gifts is to learn the art of life. Millions of people are failing to make the most of their opportunities because they are failing at that very point.

What the "best gifts" are, no one will doubt who has looked steadily into the mirror of Christ. It is "a good gift" if one has an adequate income (and who could sincerely wish for less?), but it is a better gift to have peace of mind. It is "a good gift" to have health of body (and what sane person would ever deliberately seek disease?), but it is a better gift to have health of soul.

The best gifts of all are those aspects of the mind of Christ which we have learned to admire—love, joy, peace, patience, kindness, goodness, faithfulness, humility, self-control—but even among those to whom the best gifts are clearly understood, the art of coveting is often little known. Right coveting is something of a science and something of an art. How can I fix with certainty on the thing I need? How can I keep a balance in my mind between effort and receptivity? —remembering that it is a *gift* and not an achievement, something handed to me rather than something painfully won? How can I kindle desire for the right things and overcome that fatal bias of my nature to covet the wrong things? How, in short, can I, as a student in the school of Christ, learn from him how to obey the counsel of his servant Paul and "covet earnestly the best gifts"?

The first common failing among people who do not know how to covet the best gifts is vagueness in their minds concerning the things they want. Vagueness in the aim is a common explanation of failure even in mundane ambitions. Some young men start life with a vague idea that they "want to get on," but with no clear sense of goal. If one seeks to pinpoint the spot on which their ambition focuses, they cannot give a clear reply. It is vague yearning and they never arrive. One meets them in middle life still murmuring about wanting to "get on," or wanting to "succeed," but turning in circles in a mist of their own making. Clarity in the aim is essential in all coveting. One must know where he is going or he will never arrive. Even if one got there by accident, he would still not know!

So it must be with this supreme ambition to have "the mind of Christ." That noble phrase *can* be used vaguely. The mind of Christ must be seen in its many facets, seen steadily, and seen most particularly at the point where it meets our most clamant needs.

It would sound pious and could be completely sincere for someone to look at Christ and say, "I want to be perfect," but it can be said with reverence that even that high aim needs to be seen in its multiple aspects and the desiring heart fixed on each of Christ's qualities in turn.

For precision at the point of receptivity and greater speed in spiritual progress, we would do well to get beyond vague yearnings of "wanting to be better" and focus our desiring hearts on particular aspects of Christ's mind. I need *that*. Precisely *that!* If this awful pride is to be broken in my life, I must have his humility. I will "go in" for it, as an eager boy might "go in" for physical exercises or a gawky girl might study to walk with grace. I know I cannot make myself humble. I know, if I did, I should be in danger of boxing the compass of sin and taking pride in my humility. I can only receive it as a gift from Christ and guard this given humility by the knowledge that none of it is really mine—but only his Spirit dwelling in me.

Yet I see the way of progress; I see how to put myself, by his help, at the receiving end; I see why it was so important to get "wise to myself" and recognize the order and greatness of my need; I see now with some exactness where, by faith, I can connect my need with his infinite supply and, by all the drawing power of strong desire, pull the blessing down.

To a sharp picture of the end required, strong desire must be added too. What is clear in the mind must be hot in the heart if coveting is to be of the earnest character which Paul laid down. People often see the right thing with needle sharpness, but they are cold toward it. Their desires all run after the lesser things—even evil things. With Browning they say:

> How sad and bad and mad it was—
> But then, how it was sweet!

How does one learn to covet the *best* things? Feelings are not the slave of the will. When the end is clear to the thought, and conscience adds its approving testimony, how can the whole thing be so warmed with longing that nature cries out for it and we find ourselves consumed with desire?

"Covet" is a strong word, and when Paul says "covet earnestly," he must be describing a longing almost obsessional. It may be doubted whether any people receive the mind of Christ in whom the longing for it has not become the master passion of their lives.

The better to understand the nature of coveting, let us picture it in a simple domestic setting. Imagine a little boy coveting a bicycle. He does not come under the condemnation of the Tenth Commandment because he does not covet his neighbor's bicycle; he wants a new one, all bright and shining from the shop, and he knows the exact one he wants and the exact price Dad must pay.

Day and night he lives with the thought of the bicycle. It is the theme of nearly all his conversation. He dreams of it. He aches with longing for the bicycle.

He explains to Mother how much shoe leather it will save if he only has a bicycle. He explains to Father that he will have more time for his homework because he will get home from school much quicker on a bicycle. He presses his nose to a soft round circle on the window of the shop and gazes with longing at the cycle of his dreams.

In imagination he possesses it already. Already, in his mind, he has been on many a holiday with it. He can mend punctures, read maps;

and he knows everything in the highway code which relates to bicycles. Sooner or later he will get it. Such ardent coveting seems almost always to achieve the end desired.

Or think of a housewife eager for a washing machine. Money may be short in the home, but that cannot prevent her coveting it. The characteristics of coveting, as we noticed them in the little boy, repeat themselves with trifling variation in the housewife. Early and late, she thinks of that machine. She explains to her husband that washday has always been a dread to her since they were married. She always goes to bed the night before washday gloomy at the prospect. But with a washing machine, washday would be almost a holiday! She would *enjoy* washing! All her friends have one. She knows just how to work it. The washing practically does itself. She would live longer, look younger . . . .

She will get her washing machine. It will be with her as with the little boy and his bicycle. That clear picture of the end in view and that ardent desire for it, which combine in covetousness, rarely fail to come to realization. There appear to be deep laws in the universe which open to this combination. And when the end desired is the end God desires also, *all* the resources of the universe move that way. God's power moves to God's ends. That is why one can be absolutely confident when the object of one's deep desire is to have the mind which was in Christ. We know that God wills this supreme blessing for every one of us.

A man cannot be certain that God wants him to make a fortune, or be a worldly success, or become famous. To claim God's power for these ends may lead to disappointment. God may have good reasons why (for his soul's health) a man should *not* make a fortune, or be a worldly success, or become famous. God's power works to God's ends. But God's end with man is to transform him by the renewing of his mind—and He renews his mind when He grants him the mind that was in Christ.

Our quest, therefore, at this stage resolves itself into a dual task. First, to see with clarity those aspects of the mind of Christ we most clearly lack, and secondly, to long after them with all the ardor of our nature. The character of coveting as we have made it out in a domestic setting will help us to understand it when we lift it to a spiritual plane.

The gain of looking into the mirror of Christ was that we became "wise to ourselves." The nauseating sins we could lug around and still not recognize as such were brought suddenly to view. We said to Christ within ourselves:

> Our secret sins are in the light
> Of Thy pure countenance.

Few people would feel guilty under every heading in self-examination. But no one could submit to this steady gazing at Christ and not be condemned again and again.

Each honest heart will know its own need best, but every soul by this discipline can be brought to that first requisite of all true coveting—to clarity of thought. We can see our need: the gravity of it and the greatness of it. We have not now to live another twenty years with a glaring fault which all our friends and enemies can see—and of which we ourselves are honestly unaware. Gazing into the mirror of Christ, God granted us the pain and the bliss of self-knowledge.

One man would be convicted of selfishness and another of fear, one of resentment and another of envy, one of self-pity and another of lust. In some instances it would be both—and both together.

Let a man honestly list his sins and see them for the shocking things they are.

Let him see also the answer to them in the mind of Christ. For selfishness, un-self-centeredness; for fear, serenity; for resentment, magnanimity; for self-pity, courage and joy. Let him see the graces he needs clearly and sharply; let him see them balanced with all their complementary graces in the perfect character of Jesus Christ.

Those are the things most worth having. Useful and necessary as material things are, what are they beside these?

Here is no vague yearning. This is not an anemic, oscillating desire "to be better." Here is a mind clearly seeing an objective—an objective almost as plain as a bicycle or a washing machine!

How can we long after those needed graces with ardor? By what means can we so inflame our own hearts that these, more than anything else, shall be the objects of our great desire?

Attend to them! Think about them. (Remember how preoccupied were the minds of the little boy and the housewife.) Look at these graces you need from every lovely angle. They have no other angles. Keep (so far as you are able) in the company of people who have them, and failing that, in the company of those who want them. Talk about them. Picture yourself possessing them. Constantly survey the mind of Christ and see these coveted graces complete in him.

The longing for them will grow in you. It is in their nature so to do. You were made to love these things. Sin has distorted your taste, but the appetites of your great Designer are still in you. Attend to these things and you will "hunger and thirst after righteousness."

Then study the lives of the saints. A good biography of a good man or woman is better than a novel. For one thing, it is true. For another, it will quicken all your longings after the mind of Christ. You will not doubt, as you turn the last page of the book, that God is able to give his mind to mortal man.

Is bad temper your problem? Then read of Fletcher of Madeley and learn how God took that hot-tempered passionate young Army officer and made him so even of temper and sweet of disposition that thousands of people called him "the seraphic Fletcher" behind his back, and his wife (herself a holy woman) said that she had "lived with an angel."

Is pride your deep besetting sin? Then read of George Herbert: a scholar, aristocrat, and courtier, who came to believe that to be born again was more important than to be highborn, and to haunt the court of the King of kings more rewarding than the court of the king of England. Picture him particularly on the day when he, who normally was "so trim and clean," arrived at his music meeting in Salisbury "so soiled and discomposed" because he had been down in the mud helping to unload and load again a poor man's horse. Hear his loving explanation to his highborn wife that "the aristocracy of a priest's wife was to claim no precedence over anyone," and observe how clearly he belonged to that higher aristocracy himself.

Or is it lust with you? Then read how God dealt with lust in the soul of Augustine of Hippo. It is all there in his *Confessions*. But dwell, not chiefly on his sins, but on his victories; not on his coaxing his carnal appetites, but on his receiving the mind that was in Christ.

There is no grace you covet which you cannot see perfectly in Jesus and beautifully in his saints. Get to know them: first the Master himself, and then those who stand "nearest the eternal throne." Read the Gospels. Steep yourself in the lives of the saints. There is nothing which so inflames desire for the best things as this. To the man who says pathetically: "I know what I need but I seem unable to want it," here is the answer. God uses this faithfulness in attention to inflame the heart with longing and we can respond to the Apostle's challenge and "covet earnestly the best things."

Meditation III

Look into the mirror of Christ again.
See yourself as you appear in him.
Pose this question to your mind: "What are my chief faults?"
Be unhurried and sure that you know them.
Now think on their opposite.
Is it fear? Fix on TRUST.
Is it pride? Fix on HUMILITY.
Is it whining? Fix on COURAGE.
See it sharply. See it in Christ.
Think of people you know who have this grace.
They are ordinary people—made extraordinary by God's help.
Think of people of whom you have read with this grace.
They were mortal men and women—made mighty by God's help.
See them! See them enjoying the thing you want.
Begin to pray:

O God, you did it for them.
Do it for me!
For Christ's sake. Amen.

26

HOW TO GET "WE" IN IT

THEY tell a story in the north of England of a village organist who was giving a recital on the chapel organ at a weekday gathering. He was enjoying himself immensely and pulling freely on the wind which the village half-wit was furiously pumping into the instrument, and after each item the organist would bow to the audience in acknowledgment of their applause and say: "Now *I* will play you . . ."—and named the next number.

Returning to his stool after another bow and another promise, he put his fingers on the keys but no sound came. After an embarrassed pause, the head of the half-wit appeared from behind his curtain and he said: "Let's have a little more 'we' in it!"

Oddly enough, there is a spiritual principle hidden in what the simple fellow said. It is part of the early discipline of those who would receive the mind of Christ and move from their perilous self-preoccupation to the indwelt life, to learn how to *think* with Christ, and *feel* with Christ, and *will* with Christ: how, in short, to get "we" in it.

Students of the New Testament are familiar with what are called the "we" passages in the book of the Acts of the Apostles. In several places the author moves without warning into the first person plural, and ceasing to say what "they" did, he begins to speak of what "we" did. Clearly, at those parts of the narrative, he was in the party himself. He is no longer relying on what others told him, but is speaking from personal experience. The narrative seems to gain in fullness and detail at those points, as though he was consulting his journal or "log" and writing with vividness of what he so clearly remembered. Most students of the book believe that Luke was its author, and that in the "we" passages he was traveling in the party with Paul.

We need more "we" passages in the book of our life. Indeed, the aim is that life will become all "we," and return to "I" only when Christ and self are so interpenetrated that one can no longer tell where "he" leaves off and "I" begin; to the point, in fact, where Paul himself came when he said: "I live, yet no longer I, but Christ lives in me."

If Christ is to come into our life, it is into our *thinking* that he must come. Thought is life. As a man thinks, so is he. If, then, our whole life is to be permeated by Christ, we must freely take him into our thinking, and in all our conversations with ourselves (the most important conversations we ever have) we must think double. Not yet have we reached the stage of the Apostle when we can say "I" and mean the Christ-identified life. Most of us are far from that.

But we must make our way to the new "I" by the discipline of thinking "we," by gladly forsaking our separateness, by exulting in the wonder of Christ within; by approaching all the activities of life in his partnership and by the firm mental picture of complete co-operation. Only so can this difficult notion of "Christ in me" and "I in Christ" reach reality.

A minister was walking one day on the seashore at Seahouses in Northumberland with his son. The boy had been questioning his father on a recent sermon in which the minister had sought to explain the reality of this indwelling and indwelt life.

"I can't understand it, Dad," said the boy. "How can we live in Christ and Christ live in us?"

As they walked over the beach, the minister saw an empty bottle still containing its cork.

Taking the bottle, he half-filled it with water from a pool, recorked it, and going to the sea's edge, he flung it as far as he could toward the Farne Islands. It fell in deep water and bobbed up and down.

"There it is, son!" he said. "The sea is in the bottle and the bottle's in the sea. In that strange combination, it has life and movement. . . ."

In that strange combination, we also may have life and movement. Transfigured life! Purposive movement! All that Christ meant when he said to his Father: "I in them, and thou in me."

But how can this central truth have reality in the mind of a man? Only in our thinking can this sense of merging personalities become real. We cannot walk the dusty lanes of Palestine with Christ as his disciples walked with him all those centuries ago, but if we open our minds and hearts to him, if we *think* him, if we so train ourselves that we approach all our problems and opportunities in his company, that kind of thinking will become second nature to us, and with passing time (for he is more eager for it than we are) his nature and our nature will be one.

Picture a normal day in the life of any man or woman eager for this indwelt life and not foolish enough to refuse any help which will enable them to receive their Lord.

They wake in the morning—and turn their first thought to Christ—instantly to him. The whole desire of their nature is that he will come and share their life. They face the day in his company, and in company so close that all the thinking is "we."

Such a man begins to forethink his day with Christ. He believes that the hairs of his head are numbered and that nothing of concern to him is of indifference to his divine Companion. His spirit is devout, and remains devout even though in his private conversation with his Lord he discards the language of the prayer book. He finds himself saying: "*We* have a full day before us, Lord. . . ." Step by step, he and his Lord go through the day. There is nothing of irreverence in his spirit when he says, concerning some anticipated testings of the day, "*We* shall have to be specially watchful there . . . ," or concerning other contacts rich in possibilities, "*We* must make the most of those opportunities. . . ." He thinks double. With passing months it becomes natural for him so to do. He gladly loses individuality. What began as an effort becomes half-habitual. Not only does he meet the known events of the day with Christ (having met them with Christ already in his early-morning meditations), but the unexpected happenings can be met with Christ also because to do all things with Him is now the settled practice of his co-operating life.

The people among whom this consecrated man is moving will know nothing of the secret converse of his soul. Unless they are spiritually insensitive to an astonishing degree, they will be aware of a radiance in his life, a deep serenity in his soul; but they will not know of the intimate conversations he enjoys with his Lord. Yet those conversations will be in process all the time—the hidden source of all his power. He is living the "we" life. By taking Christ resolutely into his thought and secret conversations, by giving Christ his mind and will, by gladly turning the spare moments of his day to the further intercourse of partnership, his whole mind becomes penetrated by the mind and spirit of his Lord, and with passing years, "I" and "thou" become "we," and the "I" only returns as it did with Paul: "I live, yet no longer I, but Christ lives in me."

Picture the close of any day in the life of this devout man. He reviews his day backwards. "*We* must go over the day together, Lord," he says, and together they do it. From its closing moments, they recall it in reverse. Everything is seen together. "*We* turned that occasion to advantage," the disciple murmurs (or was it the Lord who said that?). The identified life is becoming so intimate that it is not always easy to know who asks and who answers. "We have had a good day," they will often say each to the other, and the disciple will be amazed at the intimacy and condescension of his Master.

But there will be occasions—growing less frequent with passing time—when the disciple will be speaking alone. Retracing their steps through the day they will come to moments when the Lord will be dumb, and only his presence will speak, and the disciple will know that he had that incident all to himself. Contrition will rise in him and words of repentance hurry to his lips.

"I did that by myself, Lord," he will say. "I acted alone."

How quickly things go wrong with the intrusive "I." He had failed momentarily to live the "we" life. In the most exact record of his experience, the disciple will say: "In success, *we* succeeded; in failure, *I* acted alone."

With passing time, this way of thinking becomes the only way of thinking, and all life is transformed by its power. More and more does Christ come in and control his consecrated servant. The life of identification after which the longing soul aspires comes ever nearer. It would be blasphemous even to think in terms of equal copartnership. The growing soul borrows the words of the hymn writer and says: "Less of self, and more of Thee." Increasing victory over temptation proves the increasing control of Christ; the increasing control of Christ means increasing power over sin. The maturing disciple loves still to live the "we" life, but less and less does he himself contribute to the victories. His small part is diligently to hold himself open to the inflowing life of God, and though his Lord encourages him still to say, "*We* did it," his growing awareness of the relationship ascribes all the victory to Christ.

The old fable comes to mind. An elephant and a mouse once crossed a wooden bridge together and when they got to the farther side the mouse squeaked to the elephant: "*We* made that bridge shake!"

Christ encourages us to say "we." He is eager to live in our life, and we have come to believe that to have the life of God in our soul is the greatest treasure any mortal can covet.

Living the "we" life is one way to it.

It sounds simple. It *is* simple. Most treasured things are.

But this simple mental device, made habitual by practice, helps to procure that great treasure—and anyone humble enough to learn from other people could begin to use it now.

Meditation IV

(Do this as soon as you wake in the morning.)

Turn your thoughts at once to Christ.

If you wake up slowly, be content at first to have your thoughts moving in his direction.

As you become more alert, become more concentrated on Christ.

Think on his eagerness to live in your life.

Think on the conquests his coming will bring.

Invite him!—for this new clean day.

Forethink the day with him.

Develop a sense of "togetherness."

Talk with him in your mind.

He encourages you to say "we":

"*We* have a full day before us, Lord. . . ."

"*We* shall have chances of helping others. . . ."

"*We* have traps to avoid. . . ."

"*We* may have hard things to bear. . . ."

"We . . . we . . . we . . ."

Anticipate every known part of the day with him.

Glow at the thought that you are not going alone.

Resolve to be ready for any whispered service to others.

It is a wonderful partnership—but you are the junior.

Ready?

The time has come. Rise and begin.

(Some people will accuse you of undue familiarity with God. To link God's greatness with our littleness by "we" seems to them profane. Don't worry!

Many eminent saints have talked with God this way.)

27

HOW TO LIVE IN THE BIBLE

MANY people find the Bible a dull book. It is unbelievable to them that others find it the most fascinating, engrossing, and sustaining book in the world. Even if they can be constrained by a sense of duty to read a fragment of it every day, they are glad when the duty is done and they can turn with eagerness to the newspaper or to a novel.

What makes this important difference? How comes it that a book can be so forbidding to one honest person and so fascinating to another?

It must be admitted that one's convictions on the character of the book and the mental attitude in which one approaches it makes an enormous difference. If a man sincerely believes that the Old Testament is a fragmentary record of a group of unimportant Semitic tribes who lived centuries ago in Asia Minor, and the New Testament an account (largely legendary) of an unusual teacher named Jesus of Nazareth, plus the correspondence of one of his chief disciples with their early converts . . . well, the book deserves no exceptional respect and reflects little more than what the people *wanted* to believe who set the record down.

If a man believes, on the other hand, that this is, in a most special sense, the Word of God, he will count any day ill spent which does not include some time given to its reverent study. He will come to the book, not thinking first of personal enjoyment or thrill or novelty, but only of understanding, and of how best he may translate its message into life.

The convinced Christian approaches the book in this second state of mind. To him it is a unique volume. Whatever degree of divine inspiration may be attached to other Christian writings (*The Imitation of Christ, The Pilgrim's Progress*), that book is unique which contains the only record of God's incarnate life, the spiritual pilgrimage of the race among whom he was born, and the birth of the Christian church.

One's appreciation of the book is not only affected by one's conviction of its character, but by the mental attitude with which such a conviction clothes the mind. Let a man believe that the holy God did indeed inspire priest and prophet, evangelist and apostle; he may still ponder on the exact nature of the inspiration, but he cannot regard it as an *ordinary* book. He will recognize that a record so written requires divine help to be read, and he will come to his study in a quietness of spirit, with a prayer on his lips, and with an eager receptivity of mind. He will put himself to school to the book, and his critical faculties will be alert, not with questions on whether or not he is in contact with God's word (for he has settled that with himself already), but only with questions concerning how God's message relates to his present situation. He is teachable before it.

That the word does speak to each succeeding day and generation, all Christian history testifies. The Christian feels that the tooth of time gnaws all books but the Bible. It has a pertinent relevance to every age. It has worked miracles by itself alone. It has made its way where no missionary had gone and done the missionary's work. The container may be an earthen vessel (for the record is sometimes in the thought-forms and imagery of the age of its writing); but it bears the living water, which comes sweet and untainted to the thirsting souls of each succeeding age. Nineteen centuries of experience have tested the book. It has passed through critical fires no other volume has suffered, and its spiritual truth has endured the flames and come out without so much as the *smell* of burning.

Those who delight in the book therefore cannot believe that their conviction of its worth is an illusion. Has it not spoken to the souls of more than fifty generations? Has not its recurrent "rediscovery" revived spiritual religion in many ages? Has it not a depth of meaning, and a power on the conscience, and a terrible personalness unparalleled by any other book in all the literature of the world?

So the Christian believes. He speaks with profound respect of the holy writings of other great faiths. He does not deny spiritual power in them, nor that they have been a beacon to their people in the dawning of the world.

But he puts the Bible in a category by itself. It is not the first of a group; it is in a classification alone. It is not the leader of equals; it is a book apart.

How can he help, then, but study it daily; store his memory with precious fragments of it; learn its highways and its byways; make its reverent reading a prime privilege of every day . . . ? If he begins its life-long study as a duty, he prays that it may become a delight. If he is slow at first to realize that God's truth comes in different forms (poetical, historical, allegorical), he will nonetheless come to that realization and exult that it is still God's truth, in each of these variant ways. He will test all things by the person of Jesus Christ. It is the mind of Christ he wants in *his* mind. That, then, will be the touchstone in all his study of the Bible: the anticipation of God's mind, its growing clarity, its full revelation in Jesus, its imparting through the Holy Spirit to the sons of men. To imagine that he could know the mind of Christ without soaking in the book where alone it is disclosed would be folly of the first order.

So he looks steadily at the Lord he would like to resemble. So he follows John Wesley (who was an all-devouring reader) in nonetheless calling himself "a man of one book"—a book which, in a unique sense, he has come to believe is *the Word of God.*

There is something else, moreover, the devout student of the book has learned to do.

He has learned to live *in* it. By a reverent use of the imagination he has developed a method of slipping within the covers of the book and making it autobiographical. It has become alive to him in a way he finds increasingly fascinating.

Some people speak disparagingly of the imagination. They classify it in their mind with fancy, whimsy, unsubstantial speculation having no basis in fact. But imagination is one of God's greatest gifts to men.

Every great achievement has to be *imaged* first in the mind before it can be turned into reality. Alcock and Brown, the first to fly the Atlantic, flew it a hundred times in their imagination before they flew it in actual fact. It was *essential* to their success that they fly it first in imagination, or else they would never have flown it at all. They saw the waste of water roll beneath them. They saw the banks of clouds shutting them in on every side. They saw the petrol gauge as the powerful engines drank the precious fluid. They saw the compass, the occasional ships, the threat of storm. They saw it all, and themselves battling with it—meeting peril with pluck and problems with incisive judgment . . . and then Ireland, the surging crowd, the deafening cheers, and themselves the center and heroes of it all—the first men to cross the Atlantic by airplane, eight years before the gallant Lindbergh repeated their exploit. They saw it all—first in imagination. They heard it all—in imagination. The difficulties they saw in imagination, they prepared for in simple fact. The keener their imagination, the more complete their preparation. When the actual difficulties came on that perilous morning in June, 1919, they had foreseen them. They had *imaged* the whole enterprise to themselves, and they knew what they would do.

All great achievements belong, first, to the imagination. The imagination is one of God's greatest gifts to men.

Yet the first and noblest use of the imagination is, not to plan things for the future, but to run back through the corridors of time and (as Ruskin said) to call up the scenes and facts of our Lord's life and "to be present, as if in the body, at every recorded event of the history of the Redeemer." That is the first great use of the imagination: to live in the Bible; to run back through time and jostle with Peter, James, and John when they stand around the Savior; to see Lazarus coming from the tomb tearing aside the graveclothes as he comes; to hear Martha complain that she is cumbered about with too much serving; or better still, to sit with Mary and listen to the words of life.

All this you can do by imagination. The proper use of the imagination is, not to conjure up false things and foolishly believe them to be true, but to take true things and make them vivid in the life of today.

There are two chief ways of reading the Bible: to read it with or without imagination. You can read it from outside or you can read it from inside. You can come to it in a detached fashion and always be external to the book, or you can slip inside the covers and live within the divine Word itself.

When I am talking to intimate friends whose fondness for the Bible is as great as my own, I often use language concerning it which would be inappropriate, and misunderstood, and indeed quite incredible when used with other people. I say to them: "I am with Jeremiah now; where are you?" And they may say to me: "I am spending my time with Ezekiel." Or I say to my friends: "I am in prison with Paul; where are you?" And they have replied to me at times: "I am the leper whom Jesus has just cleansed." They understand me and I understand them. You see, by the use of the imagination (this divine gift!) we are both living *in* the Bible. It is wonderful to be the leper when Jesus cleanses you, wonderful to be Jairus when your daughter is raised from the dead, wonderful to be the widow of Nain when your son gets up from his bier.

Let us put the method to a test. Let us take two incidents from the Scriptures—one for men, with a man as the central figure, and one for women, with a woman in the chief role—and let us see how we can bring them to life.

Let the first be the story of Zacchaeus (Luke 19:1-10).

Read it! Read it again slowly. Raise certain questions in your own mind. Where did it happen? Jericho! Look up Jericho on the map. What is known of Jericho in the time of Christ? It was an important customs station on the principal caravan route from the East to Judea. A travel book of Palestine might easily contain a picture of an Eastern town. . . .

When did this incident happen? Only a few days before the Cross. Christ was on his way to die. . . .

What do we know of this man Zacchaeus himself? He was a *chief* publican. The chief publican in an important border town! Precisely what *was* a publican in those days? . . . Almost certainly, as the chief, he "farmed out" the taxation rights. How contemptible he must have seemed to the religious people of Jericho! Ostracized from decent society, without a doubt. He seemed a dirty, disloyal, and loathsome extortioner, with whom one would be ashamed to be caught talking in the street.

But he *must* have had an aching longing to see Jesus! Had he heard that Christ was friendly with publicans and sinners? After all, it was a quite ridiculous thing that he did—to clamber up a tree! He was no boy and he was the *chief* publican. How *keen* he must have been. . . .

Was he short of stature? It seems so. It is not *certain*. The pronoun *could* apply to Jesus. Christ could have been short and not easily seen over a crowd. But it was probably Zacchaeus who was short, and up the fig-mulberry tree he went. It is an easy tree to climb. The short trunk and wide lateral branches make it ideal for the purpose, and the perch promised all he desired. . . .

(Work at it like that. Question the narrative. Heap information together. Be unhurried in all this preparation.)

Now for the next step.

Slip, in imagination, into the skin of Zacchaeus. You are Zacchaeus and Zacchaeus is you. *Think* yourself into him. It is not really hard, and comes easily with practice. Actors have to do it on every working day of their lives, and do it so completely that they lose themselves in their parts and are still playing them when they get back to their dressing rooms.

You are Zacchaeus, feared and despised, important and contemptible —contemptible even to yourself, secretly longing to be clean. . . .

"What's that? Jesus of Nazareth is coming. Jesus of Nazareth! Isn't that the man whom Matthew followed? Is he coming here? . . . now? . . ."

So all your longing gets into your legs and you hurry to the road by which he is entering the town. A crowd is swirling round him.

"I'll have no chance to see him here. . . . *What can I do?* . . . That tree! . . ." You're up it before you think of it and the next moment the crowd is beneath you and his eyes are on your shameful face.

(Note how every detail is vivid, every sense employed. You *see* the crowd, and burn with the heat, and almost sneeze in the swirling dust, and feel the grip of the tree branch in your hand. It is on to *your* face that Jesus turns his luminous eyes, and when he says "Zacchaeus" he says "you.")

"I never get past that point," a friend who practices this method of Bible study confessed to me. "When he calls my name, everything turns into prayer."

The Gospels are rich in incidents of Jesus in touch with women— and never by a hint does he imply their inferiority as women. Let us look at him dealing with that poor crippled woman in the synagogue (Luke 13:10-17).

Follow the same method. Read it. Read it again slowly. Read it several times.

Raise questions with yourself. The woman had "a *spirit* of infirmity." Does that mean some form of possession? But no other marks of demon possession appear in the narrative. She was almost bent double. It *could* be psychological in origin, but most doctors take it as a case of *spondylitis deformans*—with the bones of the spine lacking all flexibility and rigidly bent like a crooked and unyielding stick. She could only look down. Eighteen years she had been like this.

Where did this happen? In an unnamed synagogue; Jesus is rarely mentioned in a synagogue in his later ministry.

What was the inside of a synagogue like? Did the women have special seats apart from the men? Were they at the back?

What was a *ruler* of the synagogue? He was not a priest. What status had he? . . .

(Heap all the exact information together that you can get. Avoid the fanciful, and keep as close to the text as you can. Have grounds in the narrative for the picture as you build it up. Go on what is stated and what can quite fairly be inferred.)

Now take the next step.

Become that poor crooked woman. Feel yourself badly bent over as if by an iron hand. Feel the sheer indignity of it, the stares of people (though you cannot see them), the innocent but wondering questions of little children about "that funny lady," your inability to take anything from a shelf or do your household work properly or ever see the stars. O God! And eighteen years of it!

Now set out for the synagogue that morning, seeing only the sandy burned-up path and the litter on the street . . . and feet, always feet! Even when you spoke, you spoke to feet and had to guess at the face above them.

"But there is still God, and it is the Sabbath, and to his house I will go. . . .

"A visiting teacher here this morning? Oh! Who? Jesus of Nazareth! I've heard wonderful things about him. . . .

"Sssh! The service is about to begin. What a nice voice he has . . . . *He calls me!!!* Oh! Oh, dear!! Make way, please. *He calls me!* I can only see the floor . . . and now his feet. *'You are set free from your sickness.'* He said it! He put his hands on me. And so I am. I can move. . . . I can lift myself *up*. He is looking at me. I can see his face. He smiles. . . . O God! . . . O God! . . ."

So see yourself with all the crookedness in your soul straightened, and the smiling face of God assuring you that your sickness is healed.

Meditation V

Read a few verses from the Bible each day.

Read them as early in the day as possible.

It need not be a chapter.

A little, thoughtfully read, is better than a lot raced over.

Don't read at random; read systematically.

Join one of the many Bible-reading groups. At a trifling cost, they supply selected passages and notes.

Offer a brief prayer for understanding before you read.

Take a few moments afterward to think it over.

Do it daily.

Once a week, treat one of the Gospel incidents in the way suggested.

Put yourself imaginatively in the book.

Study the whole incident.

Learn all you can about it.

Select the character you will be.

Be that character.

Live the part.

Alert every sense which is involved: touch, taste, hearing, sight, and smell.

Meet the Master—in fifty different relationships.

You want the mind of Christ.

How better can you know it than in his company?

Keep, then, in his company. Only so can you know his mind.

28

HOW TO MAKE A PRAYER PATTERN

THERE is no way to get the mind of Christ which belittles, or ignores, or scamps the disciplined practice of prayer. The way to know Christ with intimacy is to talk with him, to talk with him daily, and to talk for more than moments.

Now, prayer is conversation with God. It involves (as all conversation does) both speaking and listening, and we may mark our progress by our increasing desire to hear God speaking rather than to speak ourselves.

Many people—even professing Christians—are neglectful of prayer. They have some memorized sequence of words which they employ at the beginning and the end of the day, and it may not have varied in years. Even this is infinitely better than no prayer at all, but it is often quite immature and its unvarying form suggests no growth in their spiritual life.

Other people—who are half convinced that their slow growth in grace is due to neglected prayer—are still casual in reformation and lacking in method. The most important activity of every day cannot be left to the vagary of feeling. Every serious Christian needs a pattern or plan for praying. It need not be complicated and must not be imprisoning. But it should be plain and firm, and observed with honest constancy. Nobody has grown in the life of God who neglected prayer.

How might such a pattern of prayer be laid out?

We have already advised the wise practice of turning one's first thoughts on waking instantly to God and developing a sense of Christ's companionship in our every attitude to life: Indeed, the word "companionship" is not close enough to describe the intimacy of our Lord's indwelling, but we are learning to open ourselves to it by thinking "we" with the first thoughts of each new day.

This being done, contrive to get (as a minimum—more later!) fifteen minutes alone as early in the day as possible. A few verses of the Bible reverently read will bring us more speedily than anything else into the conscious presence of the Master, and normally it will not be hard to converse with Christ already felt as near.

The sequence of our prayer might run like this:

Praise. Adore God in your heart. Think on the *wonder* of a soiled sinner like yourself being welcome in his presence and encouraged to linger as long as you like. Exult in the knowledge that this world is not the sport of half-made men, but that God has the whole frame of things in his hands and that we live in a guarded universe. Our freedom is real *but limited.* Not even hydrogen bombs can blast the pillars of the cosmos. It is God's world—the tender, merciful God revealed to us in Jesus Christ. *Praise him!*

Thanksgiving. There is never a time when thanksgiving is completely out of place. Even in rare days of dire calamity, there is always something to be thankful for, and in normal and unclouded times there is ground for thanksgiving on every side. Let your mind run over the many reasons you have for being grateful. Health, home, love, friends, flowers, work, wholesome books, good-tempered fun, the opportunity of service, the privilege of prayer . . . . If honesty compels you to admit that you do not enjoy some of the blessings set out in this list, you can think of many more omitted here that you *do* enjoy. So just *think* on them—till the heart swells with gratitude and thanksgiving rises because it must.

Dedication. You are already a committed man or woman, and committed by lifelong vows. But it is a new day! Give yourself afresh to God. Say with Philip Doddridge, "That vow renewed shall daily hear." God is your Master, and your soul seeks no other Captain than Christ.

Guidance. Pray to be made sensitive all day to his guiding hand. Live under its gentle pressure. Thrill at the thought that you are not facing life alone. Foster the secret elation of knowing that, if some things in this day just beginning are unknown to you, they are all known to him. Learn the listening side of prayer. We must talk later of the problems of guidance and how to get it in perplexity. But we are not normally in perplexity. To sensitize our spirit to the Master's presence at the beginning of every day is the best way to be certain that we shall be guided till its end.

Intercession. Pray for others. Even this holy occupation of prayer can be soiled by selfishness, and most of the masters of prayer give more time to praise and intercession than to anything which immediately concerns themselves. Keep lists of people you know who are in special need. Keep an urgent daily list—and a weekly list as well. Mention them by name. The names could be written at the back of your Bible or diary. Do not leave intercession to the chance recollection of the moment. Probably nothing we do for others is so valuable as prayer for them. Bring method into it therefore. Pray with persistence, and God will help you to pray with passion also. Remember the sick—in body, mind, and soul; the church—at home and abroad; our leaders—national and ecclesiastical . . . remember your friends and dear ones. We must say more, later, about the special character and value of intercession, but the best way to learn intercession is to intercede. Its daily practice will teach us more than much theory. If the only way to learn to play the violin is to play it, the only way to learn to pray is to pray.

Petition. Last and least, we may mention our own requests to God. Jesus encouraged us so to do. Had he not encouraged us, we might have hesitated to include personal petition in our prayer pattern at all, and respected rather those advanced souls who cut it out altogether on the ground that God knows what is best for us and may be trusted to give it, as and when he will. But no authority approaches our Lord's. Jesus encouraged both petition and persistent petition too.

But it is last and least on our list. Prayer must be guarded from selfishness. Yet, there come times of acute anxiety in life when we cannot *prevent* ourselves pleading with God for something. Plead therefore! God would not have us dumb in such an hour. Pour it out! His ear is ever open toward his needy children's cry.

So much for *morning* prayer. Find a minimum ten minutes toward the close of the day and go to God again. In learning to get "we" into it, we are learning to run over the day backwards and pausing for pardon at the places where we failed. Confession has its inescapable place in praying, and its best place is here. Don't sleep until the day has been reviewed in the light of God. You will sleep better when your penitence has been blessed with his pardon. Then each day can begin clean.

There will be cause for much thanksgiving, too, as you review the day. All his promises have been fulfilled. You will not be able to leave intercession out. People in acute need will demand a mention in your evening prayers, as in the morning ones. You are seeking healing sleep yourself and you will seek it also for the sick and those who mourn.

Let your last thoughts of all as you sink into sleep be of God and his goodness. Sink into the thought of God even more than you sink in the bed. Rest your whole weight on him. The mind continues to work in odd ways even while we sleep. Let it work on the best things. Thoughts of trust and of peace, holding the mind in the hours of our resting, are far the best tonic for tomorrow—a tonic equally sustaining for body, mind, and soul.

A prayer pattern quickly builds itself into our life and takes on the solidarity of good habit. It soon has the regularity and naturalness and nourishment of our meals. We need not (and *should* not) limit our praying to the prayers offered in these guarded and unhurried periods at morning and evening. We may pray anywhere—in the street and as we travel, at our work and in our fun.

But let these unpremeditated prayers all be *extras,* not substitutes. Growth in the mind of Christ demands iron firmness with ourselves in our fixed periods of prayer.

We can vary the pattern as God guides us, for there are many ways to pray. But no *sustained* prayer will be in harmony with the best spiritual insight of our race if it omits adoration, thanksgiving, confession, and intercession. A pattern of prayer is not the recipe of a pudding—spoiled if one ingredient is left out. But *regular* prayers which are not built on adoration, thanksgiving, confession, and intercession are not built well.

The great and recurrent danger of our prayer life is that it will all become personal petition. "Give me . . . Give me . . . Give me . . . ." Against that we must watch hardly less vigilantly than we watch against the danger of having no prayer at all.

Meditation VI

(No prayer pattern is any use if one lacks the *desire* to pray or the will to it.

The aim of this meditation is to inflame desire and strengthen the will.)

Think of the great end of our quest—to have the mind of Christ.

Think of those who have most had his mind—their love, joy, peace.

Remember that one of the chief means by which they received the divine life was by constant conversation with God.

Face the fact that to neglect prayer is to miss the prize and to practice prayer is a chief way to secure it.

Recognize the folly of the common idea that prayer has no value unless you "feel" like it.

Ask yourself what are the deep reasons why the masters of prayer have said that God can do more with our prayers when we pray without feeling than when we pray with it.

Resolve, therefore, to keep your appointment with God whether you feel like it or not.

Constancy will bring its own reward. Firmness with yourself when feeling ebbs will bring the feeling later like a flood.

But no day without prayer!

29

HOW TO PRAY THE AFFIRMATIVE WAY

It will surprise some people that we take so poor a view of personal petition in prayer and regard its tendency to absorb all our moments of devotion as the greatest danger of our secret talk with God.

Therefore we must make clear the place petition may justly have in our prayers, and how legitimate petitions offered to God in faith cease to be petitions and become affirmations instead.

Not all personal petitions go into the same classification.

Some requests leap from our heart because they must. A man's child may be desperately ill, or the doctor may suspect a malignant growth in the man's wife, or his economic security may be seriously threatened . . . . How can a believing man help but pray? He would have to throttle himself to prevent the pleading words pouring from his lips—and God does not expect us to check ourselves in hours like these. Any theory of prayer which forbade a man's going to God in great personal need would be self-condemned. The heart would cry out against it.

But hours as dark as these are rare in life. Condemnation falls upon prayer as personal petition, not because a man in great extremity pleads with God for wife or child, but because the regular day-to-day prayers of so many people are all made up of selfish requests. They can ignore the crying needs of other people (and often people *they know*) and use all their moments of prayer in begging for material things which it is by no means certain would benefit them if they came—more money, more influence, more distinction, more worldly success. . . . Fancy being dumb about your neighbor's sick child while you fill the ears of the Almighty with earnest pleading for that lucrative contract your rival has had until now! Is prayer not demeaned by such use? Would you make the Almighty the accomplice of your selfishness? God is not indifferent to material things, for he made them and he made them good, he loves to give them to those who seek first the kingdom of God, and even then, more to the measure of their need than their asking.

But personal petitions are not always offered only for material things. They can be offered for spiritual things as well. A man pleading for the mind of Christ is offering a *personal* petition. If he breaks it up into its components and asks for love, joy, peace, patience, kindness, goodness, faithfulness, humility, and self-control, it is still personal petition. He *could* be accused of selfishness.

Yet the New Testament teaches us to "covet earnestly the best gifts" and God is glad when we want these things. It is only another way of saying that we want *him!* To discover crude selfishness in this is to be "overnice."

Let no man hesitate to seek the mind of Christ because he may be suspected of selfishness. The greatest service anyone can render to the community is to have the mind of Christ. Nothing would be more advantageous to the world than more people with the mind of Christ. It is through the channel of those who have Christ's mind that God is able to pour his power into this world. Every advance in our spiritual maturity makes us more usable by God, and no warning uttered against the danger of making all our prayer personal petition must be taken as checking the longing to have the mind which was in Christ.

It would be a good thing if, as we prepared to pray, we asked ourselves concerning any petitions we thought to bring to God, "Can I ask this in Christ's name?" That would not mean, "Can I attach that formula to the end of my prayer?" because clearly the formula could easily be attached to the most crude selfishness. But, "Is this petition in harmony with Christ's will? Can I be certain that this is what *he* wants? Is it beyond question that I can invoke the Savior's name for such a course as this?"

Concerning some things you would have, in all honesty, to say, "I don't know." Who could say with positivity that he *knew* it was the will of Christ that his business should expand?—or even that his wife should recover from her sickness? We may legitimately ask these things because we deeply want them, but it is *possible* that an expanding business might bring hidden dangers to the soul and it is *possible* that God wants that dear one in heaven. No Christian can think it a disaster to go to glory!

Concerning other things, no shadow of doubt remains. We *know* God's will. We know that he "desireth not the death of a sinner but rather that he may turn from his wickedness and live." We know that he wants to give us health of soul, the mind of Christ, love, joy, peace. . . . To wonder about these things is to wonder about something we ought never to wonder about at all. *We know!*

Now, when we are sure that a thing we want for ourselves is in the will of God, and when we have faith for it (as we ought), the prayer of petition passes into affirmation and we pray the affirmative way. A little consideration will show the rightness of this.

Suppose we are seeking God's gift of supernatural love. We have seen that love is the first fruit of the Spirit and the basis of all the rest. We have seen our need of it and lack of it. We are longing for that divine infusion in the soul which makes it possible even to love people we cannot like. Our natural impulse is to put our longing into personal petition and say: "O God, give me this love."

But that is not prayer as the New Testament teaches it.

You are sure that God is eager to give you this love. He does not need to be pressed, or coaxed, or cajoled into it. He is more eager to give than you are to receive.

Moreover, Christ said: "Whatsoever you pray and ask for, believe that you have received them, and you shall have them."

Do not *ask* for it, therefore. *Believe* for it. It is his known will. It is already coming to you. The initiative is in heaven. Only your unbelief can keep it out. Have faith for it! It is already coming to you but it will come more swiftly as you "send faith before to grasp it." Do not ask for it then, but *affirm* it. Not, "O God, give me this love," but

In Christ, I am filled with *love.*
In Christ, I am filled with *joy.*
In Christ, I am filled with *peace.*

So, by another route, we find ourselves again in our first meditation and understand the Biblical basis and psychological soundness of praying the affirmative way. When personal petition becomes sound affirmation we are wide open to God's incoming, and nothing need hinder our receiving the mind that was in Christ.

It would seem irreverent to criticize ancient modes of prayer, but many of these are irreverent themselves. We plead with God to bless us—who has been blessing us all our lives. If some of his blessing has not reached us, it is because our unbelief has shut it out. We plead with God to guide us—who has sought to guide us all our days. If on occasion we have missed our way, it is because we have not had faith for guidance.

Why *plead* in circumstances like these? Do you doubt God's willingness, his love, or his power? Affirm your faith!

"O God, thou art blessing me at this moment."

"O God, thou art guiding me by thy counsel."

Those are the facts. Believe them! Thank God that it is so. Exult in the truth of it and let realization break out into praise.

Some people confuse the prayer of affirmation with autosuggestion. They are not the same thing. Autosuggestion (as the name makes clear) centers in the self. Affirmative prayer centers in God. Autosuggestion can be used to "kid" oneself. Affirmative prayer deals only with the truth.

Even devout people sometimes stretch the prayer of affirmation beyond its legitimate use. We have no right to turn all our desires into affirmations and assert in the name of God that they are coming to pass. Before you shape an affirmation, scrutinize it again. "Is this the known will of God?" "Am I sure beyond all doubting that he means this thing?" "Does any uncertainty linger in my mind concerning its *truth?"*

When Émile Coué, of the Nancy School of Autosuggestion, visited England, some misguided person took him to St. Dunstan's, the home for blind soldiers. That phalanx of brave men, their eyes destroyed by war, sat before him and he talked. Out came his little formula. "Every day, in every way, I am getting better and better." How should it be applied here? "Every day, in every way, I am *seeing* better and better."

It was a lie!—a palpable, ludicrous, and bitter lie. They took him away. Better so! There are phases of autosuggestion which are stupid to the point of insult.

Affirmative prayer must never be dragged down to this level. To teach a poor soul twisted into a figure of eight by rheumatoid arthritis to affirm, "Because God is in me, I can move about freely," is to mingle blasphemy and banality to a shocking degree. Affirmative prayer centers in God and deals with the truth. When it hurries forward to grasp a truth not yet realized, it is never in doubt of God's intentions. It is a tried way of opening our natures to the *truth*. It is a means by which we can build facts to which we give mental assent into the deepest strata of our subconscious minds. It is one of the surest means by which we can receive the mind of Christ.

The best affirmations are made from the Bible and the hymnbook. A soul keen for spiritual progress quarries for them constantly in the Book of God and finds them also in the finest of our church hymnody. The search for them is itself a fascinating form of Bible and hymnbook study, and to have a mind stored with the wide selection of them is to be prepared for all the experiences of life.

Sometimes one must slightly change their form to make them suitable as affirmations—but in changing the form we must be careful not to change the sense.

Here are selections picked almost at random from just two writers: Paul in the New Testament and Charles Wesley in the hymnbook.

Paul

When marking the anniversary of my conversion:

"God, who commanded the light to shine, shines in my heart to give the light of the knowledge of the glory of God in the face of Jesus Christ."

When fear assails:

"I can do all things through Christ who strengthens me."

When in trouble:

"I know that all things are working together for good to them that love God."

When prayer is hard:

"The Spirit is helping my infirmities."

When seeking assurance:

"The Spirit himself is bearing witness with my spirit that I am a child of God."

When thinking of death:

"I know that if my earthly house is dissolved, I have a building, not made with hands, but eternal in the heaven."
"For me to live is Christ and to die is gain."

Charles Wesley

For a new convert:

'Tis done! Thou dost this moment save,
With full salvation bless;
Redemption through Thy blood I have,
And spotless love and peace.

For one afraid:

Faith, mighty faith, the promise sees
And looks to that alone;
Laughs at impossibilities,
And cries: It shall be done!

For one in trouble:

And all the attributes divine
Are now at work for me.

For the stimulation of prayer:

Thou art wisdom, power, and love,
And all Thou art is mine.

For one enjoying assurance:

My God, I am Thine;
What a comfort divine,
What a blessing to know that my Jesus is mine!
In the heavenly Lamb
Thrice happy I am,
And my heart it doth dance at the sound of His name.

Forethinking death:

> Through Thee, who all our sins hast borne,
>   Freely and graciously forgiven,
> With songs to Zion we return,
>   Contending for our native heaven;
> That palace of our glorious King,
> We find it nearer while we sing.

How rich the treasure may be judged by the ease with which these come to the mind.

But let every man make his own set. Memorize them! Have them on easy call. Note their character. They are all God-centered and they are true. They do not ask; they affirm. They are not pleading; they are asserting. Store them in your warm, believing heart. Select them as you need them. Murmur them to yourself and (when possible) murmur them aloud. Slowly, quietly, and thoughtfully, say them over and over again. This is to pray the affirmative way, and it can be used in our fixed prayer periods, and it can fill the odd moments of every passing hour.

Meditation VII

Be quiet before God.
Get clearly in mind the exact nature of affirmative prayer.
It is opening ourselves to receive the mind of Christ.
It is all God-centered.
It concerns things on which God's mind is clearly known.
It is offered in utter faith.
Asking, therefore, would be unfitting.
It would imply doubt of God's word or a lack of personal *faith.*
Neither doubting God's word, nor his willingness, we *affirm.*
It is happening *now.* God is doing this thing. I believe for it.
The mind of Christ is coming into my mind.

> *"My God, I know, I feel Thee mine!"*
> *He is mine, and I am His;*
> *All I want in Him I have,*
> *Life, and health, and rest and food.*
> *All the plenitude of God.*

Ask yourself what special quality of Christ's mind you are likely to need this day.

Patience? Humility? Kindness? Courage?

Affirm it! Say it quietly over and over again.

> *In Christ,* I am filled with *courage.*
> *In Christ,* I am filled with *courage.*
> *In Christ,* I am filled with courage. . . .

30

HOW TO USE IMAGINATION IN PRAYER

WE have already spoken of the power of imagination. We have recognized that those people are mistaken who disparage it and who appear to doubt whether it is a divine gift or not. We believe it to be one of the biggest boons God ever gave to men.

Many psychologists regard the imagination as more powerful than the will. They believe that if the will is set in one direction but the imagination is firmly held in another, the imagination will ultimately win. Part of the secret of progress in the spiritual life is to harness the imagination in the quest for the mind of Christ.

We are already beginning to develop our powers of imagination in Bible study. Incidents in the Gospels are becoming more vivid to us as we slip into the unfolding narrative and live in the skin of Zacchaeus, or in the woman with the crooked back, or in any other.

We need now to employ imagination in prayer also.

Picture yourself already possessing the graces you have learned to crave. *See yourself* enjoying those aspects of the mind of Christ of which you stand in sharpest need. Harness the imagination to this high quest, and what the will cannot do in its feebleness, the imagination (used by the Spirit of God) will finally bring to pass. *Picture the prayer fulfilled.* Link imagination with affirmation. Do not merely *say* it. *See* it. Hold in your mind, in those moments of your praying which are given to personal petition, the clear image of yourself made anew by Christ. See it with precision and sharpness. The proud you, really humble. The fearful you, truly trusting. The resentful you, fully forgiving. Just hold the picture there! It is only a matter of moments in your praying. The length and strength of your prayers, as we have agreed, must never be given to personal petitions, however lofty. The claims of intercession are too great for that. Yet this discipline of moments, if it is observed *daily,* can be infinitely rewarding. Power comes into prayer when imagination is used in this way. Charles Wesley was bold to say of the Holy Spirit that He was "drawn by the lure of strong desire." He is indeed. And when the coveting which Wesley describes as "strong desire" is linked with faith and expressed in affirmation, and when imagination is harnessed also by a picture of the realized end held vividly before the eye, all the doors are open and the power of God floods in.

And all this for a few moments a day.

See it done! Link affirmation and imagination together and you are giving your mind to Christ in a way which makes it possible for Christ to give his mind to you.

The transformation proceeds apace.

Meditation VIII

(This is hardly a meditation, in the sense in which we are using the word here. It is just a method of using a few moments a day to employ imagination in receiving the mind of Christ.)

Except in times of acute concern, be careful to give only a minor place in your prayers to personal petition.

But because we believe that if we have the mind of Christ our service to God and to others will be enormously enlarged, do not think it sinfully selfish to seek it.

But do not *ask* for it. Knowing that God is already giving it to you, open yourself to its inflow by affirmation. Assert in faith that you have it *now*.

That it may more clearly and swiftly appear, *see* it (with the eye of imagination) already in you and see it this way!

After each affirmation (either in your set times of prayer or in the unexpected moments you can find in the day) see yourself with the grace you seek. Do not merely *say* you have it. *See* it within. Hold the picture of the completed thing vividly in your mind's eye. Observe it clearly, and with all the gladness and gratitude of realization.

One full minute at the right place in your prayers, and never left out—however busy the day—would work wonders. In less than a year you would not be the same person.

31

HOW TO PRAY FOR OTHERS

THERE has been a serious danger overshadowing this quest for the mind of Christ, a danger of which we have been aware from the outset. It is the danger of becoming too self-concerned and self-engrossed. A man does not need to pursue a low end to become selfish. He may aim to be a hero or a saint and still fall into the pit of selfishness. It is not the moral quality of the end which determines the selfish character of the occupation, but the fact that self is central and self is first. Even the high ambition to have the mind of Christ *could* be self-defeating if we sought it for ourselves alone. The serious seeker of the mind of Christ is secured against the peril of selfishness just so long as the strength and persistence and passion of his prayers are all for other people.

There is no human glory in intercessory prayer. The popular preacher may have his admiring crowd. He stands in a pulpit, "high and lifted up." The able evangelist, organizer, administrator, reformer, and social worker all move in a circle of those who know their fame and may envy their skill. But the intercessor (though he be more mighty than all the rest put together) receives no human admiration or applause. Those who benefit most by his titanic toil are often quite unaware of the channel of their bounty. He works in secret and his enormous service to the community is known only to God.

Friends may collect his letters after his death (as did the friends of Forbes Robinson) and the secret will be out. Or people will heap together their recollections of such a man and publish a memoir (as they did of Praying Hyde). But it is all posthumous. He has prayed in secret and God heard him in secret. The "open" rewards which Jesus promised to the secret intercessors are not rewards which the world would heed. Their great reward is that they have more of the mind of Christ. It came almost as a by-product. They were not consciously seeking love, joy, peace, patience . . . they were seeking a blessing for someone else—a stranger maybe. Intercession became the important business of every day with them. Spending the secret hours asking a blessing for others, they open themselves to the greatest blessing of all. Christ comes and lives in them.

All who are advanced in spiritual things are convinced of the importance of intercessory prayer. Many students working on the borderlands of human knowledge have expressed the opinion that the great discoveries of the next half century will not be in the physical world (which has yielded so much in the century and a half now past), but in the mental and spiritual realm, in the contact of mind with mind and soul with soul. Medical men are now so fully convinced that the state of the mind affects the health of the body that whole categories of disease are now classified as psychosomatic or partly psychosomatic. The disease is in the flesh but it did not enter the body by a germ or a virus; it came in by a thought, an anxiety, a diseased imagination, a conscience distress, a burning memory. And if disease can come in that way, so can health. Every minister with any length of ministry has known people who have snapped out of invalidism by a spiritual experience. Divine healing (in that sense of the word) is so common as to be unremarkable. It happens a hundred times a week.

Yet it is not there that the most remarkable discoveries of the future are likely to occur. Evidence accumulates that mind touches mind at a deeper level than the conscious and without physical nearness at all. People often find themselves thinking of those who are thinking of them. Thoughts are transferred. Scientists have amazed (and then appalled) us during the last two decades by unlocking vast power within the universe, but it may be that vaster power is still to be tapped on the spiritual plane and that devotion is the "science" of it and intercessory prayer the way of its coming. Prayer reaches out to all the resources of God. Faithful prayer is a conduit opened to the spiritual world by which its power may flow into this. Concentrated prayer can often move the prayerless to think on God and tremulously open themselves to the inflow of divine power. People without faith, brought into the company of believers and made the subject of silent prayer, have felt the pressure on them of spiritual influences and become half aware of a world whose existence they had scornfully dismissed. It made them doubt their doubts. Revivals of religion owe more to the power of prayer than ever they do to the natural gifts of human agents. The world has yet to see the marvels that could be wrought by costly, concentrated, widespread, and believing prayer.

A ministry of intercession is probably the crowning ministry of the Christian life. While it cannot be learned too early in life, there are senses in which it grows more powerful with passing time and most powerful in old age. It may, indeed, be the special ministry God would ask of the old.

The years have brought some wisdom and mellowness. The years have brought, alas, their griefs and heavy sorrows—and therefore their understanding and sympathy. One cannot run about as much as in the former years. Is life over then? Is it a case of just quietly waiting until one's name is called?

No! Life's greatest ministry is still open. One has time and equipment for it that one did not have before. Bend your strength to this! Join the thin ranks of the great intercessors! Rise each day to pray! A lifetime of experience has prepared you for this. Undazzled by the false glare of the world, set free from crude ambition, with eternity in full view to correct the false values of earth, *pray*. By way of adoration, confession, and thanksgiving, pass swiftly to intercession. Pray for others. Give the best thought and time and strength to this. In heaven you will see that nothing you did in life's unfolding story was so influential, and lasting, and truly rewarding as this.

There have been many men named John Smith—and not a few of them famous. But the one who comes most frequently to my mind is the one who was for years a master at Harrow School and who, in the days of his retirement, spent his long mornings in an occupation which the few people who knew about it found somewhat mystifying. He gave the freshest hours of his day to the old Harrow School Lists and *Whitaker's Almanack*. From one to the other he turned in concentrated study and then in concentrated prayer.

What was the old man doing? Had he grown senile?

No! He was rendering his greatest service to the boys who had passed through his form. He was following their careers the best way he could, and wrapping them round with his prayers. He wanted them to be the best for God and men in whatever situation they found themselves, and he helped them in this secret way. Many a man in some responsible and perhaps lonely post must have felt all his desires to do the right thing strengthened in strange ways and by a ministry of which he was all unaware.

People who make intercession the main or one of the main tasks of their lives can seldom be brought to talk much about it, but on the few occasions I have induced them to speak, they have all spoken of the rich rewards it has brought to themselves. I need hardly say of a service so unselfish that it is not undertaken with that end in view, but being undertaken for others, they declare that glorious consequences accrue in their own souls. They do not deny the time it takes, nor the cost in concentration, nor the setting aside of other things; but they speak of being braced by it, released, and made inwardly free in the spirit. Nor is it hard to understand why this should be. A feature of almost all nervous illnesses is a terrible preoccupation with oneself. How wrapped up in themselves all neurasthenics are! It is self, self, self—morning, noon, and night. Their feelings, fears, and failings; their burdens, pains, and griefs. They lapse into a kind of mental cannibalism. No thought goes out to stay out. It returns to feed on the self.

But those who spend their strength on intercession have built a granite wall against "nerves." Their thought is truly outgoing. Their desiring heart is fixed on the good of others. No wonder they feel released in the self and inwardly free. The very secrecy of their service secures them from self-deception. Any tasks which involve publicity and invite the applause of others also involve the uncertainty in any sensitive soul that some admixture of motive may be in them. They reason with themselves: "I *may* be doing it for the sole glory of God and the service of men. I think I am, *in the main*. But does not ten per cent of my nature covet the approval of men? I certainly miss the approval when it does not come!"

Secret intercession involves no dangers of perplexities of that character. *It is known only to God*. It is the most unselfish occupation imaginable. It can be practiced for years with the most glorious consequences without another human soul knowing through what human channel that stream of blessing flows.

But God so loves it that he rewards it richly; he develops in his intercessors a well-knit soul, strengthens them in un-self-centeredness, and imparts the mind which was in Christ. The grace grows with passing time. They use their bit of unselfishness this way, and he makes it more. They persist, and he makes it mighty. They are the powerful people in all communities, though they may be completely unmarked by the social, cultural, and religious leaders and never mentioned in the press.

If a man or woman felt led of God to give himself in a special way to intercession, how should he go about it?

With *method,* of course. So high a task (as we have already noticed) could not be left to the vagary of feeling. To blunder into God's presence and just chat about people who chance to cross our mind is unthinkable. We need a prayer list. Names could not be added lightly to it—even though some people (unaware of the costly nature of this service when seriously undertaken) lightly ask for it. The compilation and variation of our prayer list is an important task in itself—the list for *every* day, the *urgent* list, the intercessions for one day a week or one day a month.

It should always be *unhurried*. Mental breathlessness and prayer do not go together. If in the honest busyness of life a man can only give a limited time to intercession, he ought still to come at it as though he had all the time there was. Some busy people are willing to cut out less important occupations or cut down their sleep to secure more time for intercession. Some retired people give hours a day to it and make it the main ministry of their life.

It will not be resented if I suggest that there is a certain *technique* about it.

Always, in prayer, the main concentration is on God. Think of God: his greatness, glory, purity, power . . . and on his vividness and accessibility in Jesus. Mind wandering may make it hard on occasion to have that vivid awareness of God which we seek, but let the time go by until you know that you are there. Concentration in prayer becomes easier with passing time, though the testimony of the saints appears to be that we can be attacked by mind wandering even in the advanced school of intercession.

With the sense of God vivid to your mind, take a name from your list. Think of the person. See him! See him vividly in his situation and need. Do not dwell on the details of his sin or sickness, and certainly do not try to reproduce the "feel" of it in yourself. Think of him, rather, as God could make him: *whole* in body, mind, and soul.

Now draw the awareness of God (in his power and readiness to bless) and your awareness of the person you are praying for (in his need and inability) *together* in the crucible of your loving and believing heart. Hold them together, as long as you can. A full minute or more. Fuse them in the flame of your affection. Small as your love is beside God's, it will seem like the solder of the joint. At times you are almost aware of the union effected. That is the moment to put your request, or claim it in faith, but often you will be glad *not* to particularize your desire for the one you are praying for. It is enough that you serve as the channel between. Let the needy soul be open to God and he is open to perfection; infinite wisdom and infinite love will work out God's perfect will in him. Your high ministry has been to offer a way between.

Now, when intercession is seen in that light, its costly character becomes clear; costly in time and costly in concentration. It will be plain that this quality of praying cannot be scamped. Running your eye quickly down a prayer list will seem almost meaningless. Some will feel that it is so demanding a ministry that they cannot undertake it in any large way.

Let them do what they can—so long as it really be for others. Nothing is too large and nothing too small.

But there will be those who read these lines and feel the call to make this their main ministry. An invalid can do it. The bedridden are not shut out. The old often have both the experience and the time. It is probably the most effective and the most neglected ministry in the modern church. As an angel looks upon a large city today, the powerhouses have no belching chimneys. The powerhouses are the homes and the churches of the mighty intercessors.

Only a fraction of the consequences of this prayer becomes obvious. It is true that as we pray for people God sometimes tells us things we can *do* for them which will help him to answer our prayers. It is well that we note those things at once and get them done. But often there is little or nothing we can do. To get God into the situation by another channel is the greatest thing of all. Sometimes months and years go by without any obvious gain. It is not often like that. But the possibility is part of the discipline and testing of this high ministry. Go on! While you are sure that your prayer is in harmony with God's purposes, never give up. He is working harder than you—but human nature is obdurate stuff. Your own is! But if you leave off praying, you close a channel to the stream of God's power. "God forbid," said Samuel to the stubborn Israelites, "that I should sin against the Lord in ceasing to pray for you." It is a solemn thought that we can sin against God by ceasing to pray for people whom he has laid on our heart. We might well say with Samuel, "God forbid!"

How does God lay a need on our heart?

We have, of course, a special responsibility to the members of our families and the circle of our friends. To be mightily concerned for the religious awakening of others and indifferent to our own people would be sad and wrong. But prayer offered *only* for our own family (and particularly for material things) can be selfishness once removed, and we need ever to be on guard against that.

God lays concerns on our *hearts* when we kindle at the news of someone's great need or of some noble cause languishing for want of interest and help. It takes *hold* of us. Perhaps our past experience and sorrows move us to identify ourselves with that need. We put ourselves in imagination in that suffering person's place, or on that lonely mission station, or by that valiant fighter for righteousness. The pity, and the love, and the purity of God ache inside us. We want to *help.*

Help then! Help by prayer! As God guides you, help also by service. But—against all the convictions of those "practical" people who never think that one is doing anything unless one is running around—you help most by deep prayer. It changes the mental atmosphere. It opens up the conduits of spiritual power. It brings in dynamite to men who have been working with cold chisels. Properly employed, nothing is so mighty as prayer.

Oddly enough, one group of people we ought always to pray for is those we kindle *against.* Only saints and the bovine can say that there is no one they dislike, and it was not always true of the saints.

Some people have given us great cause to dislike them. They may have injured us, by deed or word, deeply and irreparably. It is hard *not* to hate them.

God has a special concern that we pray for them. He is wanting to rid us of the mild dislike or burning hate, and this is one way to it. He uses prayer as a filter. The very *effort* to pray for them will help us. The prayer will help us even more. You cannot hate people you pray for. The two things will not live together in the same heart. As you compose your mind to prayer, something happens in your thought.

If you are disliking them without a cause (and we often *do* dislike people without a cause) prayer brings you to that realization. If you are disliking them for a trifling cause (their manner, or some petty annoyance they gave you), the whole thing *looks* trifling in the light of God. You feel ashamed of your own pettiness. If you are disliking them for some major injury, you can see the thing without exaggeration. You can even see in God's light how that evil thing might have disguised itself as good to them. You see the weakness of their character, and you remember that you are a sinner yourself.

Pray to love them. God has in his gift a supernatural love by which the Christian can even love people he does not like.

Once this is given, prayer is not impossible. It is not even hard.

Pour it out.

Christ prayed for his murderers and you want the mind of Christ.

Pray for those who have injured you. It is probably the greatest triumph of intercessory prayer.

Meditation IX

Set aside time each day in prayer for others.

Have a list of those people and causes for which you feel a special concern.

Get alone and go to God for these great needs.

Don't worry if most of the time goes realizing the sense of God's nearness.

When you are consciously in his presence, hold out the needs of those on your list and on your heart.

One by one, just place them before God—reverently, thankfully, confidently.

When you are praying for someone's conversion, pray with Teresa:

> *Recall these dead to life, O Lord. Lazarus didn't ask Thee to raise him up but Thou didst raise him out of love for a sinful woman. Behold a still more sinful woman at Thy feet.*

When you don't know what to ask, pray with Catherine of Genoa:

> *Lord, I know not what is best for this child of Thine; but Thou knowest.*

When you are weighed down with someone's great need, still go on (as George Macdonald said) "thinking of God and them together!"

32

HOW TO GET GUIDANCE

We have already referred in these studies to "the listening side of prayer," and it is important that we now turn our whole mind toward it. We are not using all the means available to us for knowing the mind of Christ if we do not learn to *listen* to him and do it in every day we live.

Some people find it hard to believe that the great God of the universe is willing to enter into fellowship with men and women and to convey his meaning to mortal minds. They think it possible that God has a will for the world as a whole, but the idea that the concern of the Almighty descends to the details of individual lives is repugnant to them. But no Christian shares that view! "God is great enough," says the Christian, "to manage the universe and take a Father's personal care of his child. The hairs of our head are all numbered." Consequently the Christian finds no difficulty in believing in the personal guidance of God and is concerned only to learn how he may best put himself in the way to receive it. The fact that the term "guidance" has been used of God lightly and superstitiously and even falsely makes no difference to the reality of this experience. For the Christian, the question is not *whether* God guides, but *how* God guides.

God guides in various ways: through the Bible, through our reason, through the Church, through circumstances, by our conscience, and by an inner light or voice. Some uncertainty may attach to any one of these ways taken alone, but when they corroborate each other, no doubt need be felt.

There are wide areas in life in which God's will is not in any question at all. The Ten Commandments have put it beyond doubt in whole sections of human conduct. A man professing to wonder whether God permits him to indulge in sexual looseness is either a conscious hypocrite or a poor self-deceiver who has so blunted his conscience by dwelling on his "peculiar circumstances" that his conscience no longer works in swiftness and accuracy. A man does not need guidance about keeping his marriage vows. He only needs strength. Yet it would be fair to admit that there are other (though less important) areas of conduct on which the Bible gives no precise guidance, or such guidance as it gives on principles is capable of genuine difference in interpretation. Yet the Bible remains a prime source of God's revealed will—most particularly in its record of the life and character of Jesus Christ.

God guides through our *reason*. It is true that our reason can become our accomplice in opposition to God, and we may even employ it to "disprove" the One who gave it to us. But that is its abuse! When we think *with* God, and "lay our reasonings at his feet," he quickens all our powers of intellect and guides us through the processes of our thought. But sometimes, and by other methods of guidance, he carries us far beyond the reach of reason and even in opposition to it, though one must have some maturity in spiritual things to understand these experiences when they come. When Paul was in Mysia in A.D. 50 all his reasoning directed him to Bithynia (Acts 16:7). It was a populous area, needing and inviting the gospel, and the best judgment of that master missionary mind pointed that way. Paul could not know (and no man alive could have known) that Bithynia and its area was soon to become a half-burnt-up desert and the whole center of civilization to move farther west. God knew! Against all Paul's reasoning, He constrained him not to go to Bithynia but to go to Troas and thence to Macedonia. When Paul went to Macedonia, he went to Europe, and it was the eventual triumph of the gospel in Europe which was to make Christianity a world faith. So human reason by itself is not enough—not even the consecrated reasoning of a great apostle!

God guides through the *Church*—in her accumulated and age-old wisdom, and in the living Christian fellowship as well. A man can diligently read his Bible, and say his private prayers, and use his reason, and still become a crank. In the vast number of Christians that there are in the world, not many *do* become cranks, but it can and does happen. We need the discipline and correction of collective spiritual experience. The Christians (and there were a good many of them at one time) who took Christ's word about "becoming as little children" quite literally and forsook (some of them in their fifties) their daily work and just played games all day long, went tragically and ludicrously wrong. The Church through the ages has often had to deal with aberrations like that. We need her wisdom to keep us from repeating past errors. The fact that the Church has herself grown cold at times (and even corrupt) does not mean that her collective wisdom is to be lightly set aside.

Moreover, something of her wisdom is conveyed to us in the living fellowship. A man who feels some constraint upon his spirit to do a daring thing for God, and believes the constraint to have a divine origin, would be well advised to seek the counsel of his consecrated Christian friends. "I feel that I should give up my position at home—influential for good though it is—and go abroad as a missionary." How can he be sure that this is not a quixotic decision?—an escape from routine?—a blindness to the Bible word that God prefers obedience to sacrifice?

He can pray, but he needs also the prayerful judgment of others. Let them be advanced in spiritual things themselves. Let them be unhurried in their waiting on God. Let them read his mind, so far as they are able, and by their God-guided questions help him to read his own mind and discover his motives. People who are unwilling to submit to the affectionate scrutiny of the fellowship in that way are in grave danger of error and some of them have gone tragically wrong.

God guides through *circumstances* also. We do not fully understand how God influences events, but nobody with any length of Christian experience doubts it. Doors close and doors mysteriously open. Odd encounters occur which seem entirely fortuitous but which influence the whole of our lives. We pick up a little magazine ("by chance," we might say) as Schweitzer did, and our life takes a new and wonderful direction. We look back over the years and we know that we have been strangely guided. With a deeper meaning even than Hamlet intended, we say: "There's a divinity that shapes our ends."

Yet guidance to be guidance must not be seen only in retrospect. While we gladly concede that we are often unconsciously guided, we normally feel the burden of decision in the time of decision itself. We are grateful for the providential happenings which "head" us in the right direction, but we often wish we could read God's signals more clearly and have more assurance in the hour itself.

God guides us also in our *conscience*. Though there is a natural hesitation today to describe conscience without qualification as "the voice of God," it is nonetheless a witness within us to the best that we have ever been taught. Moralists have pointed out that the *content* of conscience varies in different communities, and what the conscience approves in one place it condemns in another. But it is easy to exaggerate all that! Man seems always to have known, as a legacy from his Maker, that the truth is to be preferred to a lie and kindness is better than cruelty. Yet there is wide variety among men in the standard of sexual morality. Moreover, the area in which one is expected to exercise morality is widely varied too; many primitive people suppose that one's duty only requires that virtue be displayed to fellow tribesmen or co-religionists. People outside the clan or the faith can be treated how you wish. It is part of the service of the higher religions, and of Christianity in particular, to make every man a neighbor and every soul one's spiritual kin. It is the *educated* conscience which God is able to use most dependably in guidance, the conscience educated from kindergarten to graduation in the school of Jesus Christ.

God guides, then, in all these ways. It is important to notice that he never overlays our personalities. We can accept or reject the counsel which he gives. He respects the freedom which he granted us and suffers us to ignore his guidance if we will. How clearly his mind has come to us through Bible, Church, and conscience may be judged by the fact that with all the varied interpretation of scripture, and all the different denominations within the Church, and all the millions of individual consciences, there is *only one major matter of conduct* on which Christians still disagree: on whether or not a Christian man may go to war.

That in itself is a remarkable thing. It proves that the common complaints of unbelievers about "being able to prove anything from the Bible," or the divided state of Christendom making it "impossible to understand *what* these Christians believe," or that "respect for the individual conscience lands us in chaos," is just not true.

Over nine tenths of life we do not need guidance. We have it already. The will of God is clear before us. On most mornings in his year a man may arise and greet the day with no uncertainty about his course. God has charted the way for him. He has only to steer by the sun.

Where, then, does the listening side of prayer come in and how does it work?

As one advances in spiritual maturity, the important decisions of life are less and less between good and evil, and more and more between the higher and the lower good. A man who fixed himself on Christ in his youth and has strengthened his early choice by years of consistent living is still subject to temptation, but he is not *prone* to fall. He feels no need for guidance concerning the revealed will of God.

He feels the need to remain *sensitive* to that will. He knows how the conscience can coarsen in the world of commerce. He knows that in some areas of business life there is an atmosphere which dims the spiritual vision, and he prays each day for piercing sight and quick responsiveness to the pressure of God's guiding hand.

And now and then he comes to a crossroad and does not know which way to go. It is not a clear case of right or wrong. If it were, he would know what to do and only need the grace to do it. It could, conceivably, be a matter of spiritual inconsequence. But he does not think so! God has a will for him in this matter. How can he discover that will? The Bible does not give him a ruling on it; the Church could not legislate in cases like this; to the conscience it appears a matter of moral indifference, or if there is some refinement of difference, it is too subtle to make out. Reason is baffled, and as both the possible doors remain open, circumstances do not decide the issue either. What can a man do, then?

He can appeal to the inner light.

The old Quakers—who made much of the inner light—believed that God would come to any man's aid in this dilemma and show him the way to go. The technique they taught was simple. Be quiet before God. Make quite sure that the matter is not already settled by the normal means which reveal God's will: i.e., by the Bible, Church, or conscience. Think the thing through. Look at all the related facts as impartially as you can. Do not rush the decision. Let the subconscious mind handle the problem for a day or two if possible. Then, in the quietness, submit to this test.

See yourself with the eye of imagination taking one of the possible ways. *See it!* Watch yourself doing it. "There I go! I've fixed on that!" Hold the picture in your mind for some moments and then let it fade.

Be quiet before God again.

Now see yourself doing the *other* thing; plainly and vividly, picture it happening. "There I go! I've fixed on *that!*" Hold that picture in your mind for some moments and then let it fade.

On one or other of those paths, so the old Quakers believed, *a deeper peace would rest.* The operative word is the word "peace." Not thrills or gladness, necessarily, but *peace.* It might even be painful, but it would still have the peace.

Go by the peace! Take that as your guided way. If there is no difference in the degree of peace, conclude that the decision is spiritually unimportant. It does not matter which way you go.

But if the decision troubled your mind and demanded this test, it is almost certainly one path rather than the other.

And God will tell you which path by his peace.

Meditation X

(This is not intended as a regular spiritual exercise. Our normal morning Bible reading and prayer undertaken with seriousness have sensitized us to God and his will. We start each day so alert to him that when [as Isaiah said] our "ears shall hear a word behind us, saying, This is the way, walk ye in it," we *do* hear the word, and not only hear but obey. This special "test of the peace" is for the rare times of serious uncertainty, when the appeal to all the normal ways of God's guidance has not settled the matter, and when our best and clearest thoughts still leave us unsure.)

Wait before God.

Let all sense of haste and tenseness go.

Just look to him and wait.

As the sense of his nearness grows stronger, and what *you* want is no longer pulling at your will, lay the issue quietly at his feet.

Don't argue or plead. Just put it down before him.

"Am I to go *this* way, or *that* way—or (conceivably) a third way? Tell me, Lord!"

Now employ your imagination in the way the Quakers teach.

Travel each road in turn. See yourself going: first here, then there.

Where did the deeper peace rest?

Go by the peace!

33

HOW TO GET MORE TIME

It will seem to some readers of this book that the new demands I am making on their time are so large that they cannot meet them. They may feel, for instance, that the meditations I commend will absorb more moments than they can afford, and they will be tempted to drop the whole enterprise as a thing beyond their reach.

They are mistaken.

It is worth more than all the time it takes. If God is willing to live in our lives, is there not something almost blasphemous in mortals' wondering if they can afford the time it takes to let him in? What would it be worth to the people we live with, and to the wider world, to offer God another unimpeded channel for his power to flow into the counsels of men? What would it be worth to ourselves to have the secret of peace and poise, gladness and gratitude, and to shine with the unaffected radiance which is the outer glow of that inner life?

No time would be too much time. Whatever we give to God would come back enriched a thousandfold.

Tagore once told this parable:

I had gone a-begging from door to door in the village path, when thy golden chariot appeared in the distance like a gorgeous dream and I wondered who was this King of all kings! . . .

The chariot stopped where I stood. Thy glance fell on me and thou camest down with a smile. I felt that the luck of my life had come at last. Then of a sudden thou didst hold out thy right hand and say, "What hast thou to give me?"

Ah, what a kingly jest was it to open thy palm to a beggar to beg? I was confused and stood undecided, and then from my wallet I slowly took out the least little grain of corn and gave it thee.

But how great my surprise when at the day's end I emptied my bag on the floor to find a least little grain of gold among the poor heap. I bitterly wept and wished that I had had the heart to give thee my all.[1]

[1] Rabindranath Tagore, *Collected Poems and Plays of Rabindranath Tagore* (New

If we give God a moment, he will turn it to gold; but if we give him an hour, what then—and if we learn to live all the time with him so that our thoughts turn eagerly toward him in all the free moments of our day, how complete the transformation, how wide the service, and how great the bliss!

Of course, the dedicated life takes time, but when good habit has built these meditations into our lives, only two occupations take much time (intercession and service), and even then just so much as God desires.

If the pattern of our present living does not allow the time it takes, we must *make* time, and time is made by the pruning of unnecessary occupations and by the quiet but resolute use of those unexpected moments which every day brings.

Go over your days in the light of God and see what you could cut out. Do not attack your time of healthy recreation if God assures you that that is not excessive. Look rather at the time lost each day, not in the friendly courtesies of common life, but in idle talk; in turning the newspaper over and over again when you have already announced that there is "nothing in it"; in looking at television; in listening to the radio, just on the chance that something good might turn up. Thousands of people who declare that they "haven't a moment to spare" in their breathless days are wasting hours like this. Charles Darwin's son said that his father's great secret was that he knew the difference between ten minutes and a quarter of an hour. There need be no tenseness in this quiet salvage of odd minutes. In a life so used, the years are short and the minutes are long.

It may even be necessary to treat some things with studied neglect until the practice of the presence of God is made a fixed part of our mental life. One of our leading violinists has explained her eminence in music by that means. She said that she did it by "planned neglect."

> I used to go to my room in the morning, make my bed, straighten the room, sweep the floor, dust, etc., etc. . . . but the violin didn't go forward. I resolved, therefore, on "planned neglect," to neglect everything until my practice was done. That was how I achieved.

York: The Macmillan Company, 1946), p. 24. Used by permission of the Macmillan Company.

God will not allow us to neglect anything essential, but he will so recast our priorities that we shall place the practice of the presence of God before everything else. Some things may go for good from our lives, and we shall be better for their going. Other things will take the minor place which is their fitting niche. But first things will be first. The great end of our being will be achieved: intimacy with God and a high usefulness to him in all his enterprises in this world.

Having pruned our days of unnecessary occupations and reduced to a minor role those occupations which have magnified their importance, we shall steadily build the habit of using for our high purpose the unexpected moments which each day brings. There is no doubt that each day brings them, even in the busiest life. Even if we already use our regular travel time in wise ways, there are times when we are all kept waiting. The bus, train, car, or plane is late. Some people fume at these delays. How dare it be late! But it is! And inconvenient though it may be, the fuming will only make things worse. Our nerves fray and we lose all poise.

Turn your mind over to God at once. Here is an unexpected opportunity to open yourself to the inflow of his peace. Think of it. Feel it coming in. Let it *rule* in your heart.

Or somebody keeps you waiting for an appointment. Or there is a long delay in the traffic. Or an interview is cancelled at the last minute. Most days bring some moments unexpectedly free. Use them quietly. Be ready at once to employ them in this wise way. The mind will not remain empty, if you do *not* use them well. Odd fantasies will float across the mind if you give no direction to your thought at all. Some of those fantasies are foolish, and some are spiritually debilitating, and some are positively dangerous. Nor can these foolish or dangerous images be excluded by "keeping the mind blank." They will be excluded only by something positive already in occupation. Have, then, in the antechamber of your mind, the thoughts you need—of God and his purposes, both through you and in you. Be ready to use such meditations as I have commended, and they will open your nature to him. Be glad to turn your full mind to the One who increasingly becomes the background of all your thinking—even in those hours when your conscious mind is concentrated on mundane things.

So will the "lost" moments of your day prove to be the moments of greatest gain, and you will join the rare company of those who do not mind being kept waiting because they make the wisest use of extra moments as they come.

Frank Salisbury, the artist, was once commissioned to paint the portrait of Bishop Brindle. As he studied that holy face, he learned to love it. Indeed, in the end he painted two portraits; one for those who had commissioned it and one for himself. It has hung on his own walls ever since.

He learned the secret of the bishop's serenity in a strange way. There was a misunderstanding between them over the hour of one of the sittings, and the busy bishop was kept waiting hours.

Yet when Mr. Salisbury came, he was quite unruffled. If it were possible, he seemed more lustered than usual with the light that burned in him. He gently put all the expressions of regret aside and quietly said (as one Christian man may to another): "I never mind being kept waiting. It gives me more time for prayer and meditation."

First, prune your days and cut out or cut down (as God directs you) all unnecessary things. Use the time thus salvaged for higher ends.

Secondly, quietly appropriate all the loose and unexpected moments of the day. Know beforehand what you will do with them. Prayer and meditation are always possible. Of other uses of those salvaged moments, I want to write next.

Meditation XI

(Twice a year—on your birthday and on January 1, if they are not too close together—go over with God your use of time. Time is, in some senses, the great equality. Another man may live longer than you live, but there are twenty-four hours in your day as well as his. It is God who lends you breath. You are answerable to him for your use of time. Don't fritter it. *Shape* your days. Use the hours. Use them well.

No day is well spent which does not include some time given to communion with God. Learn to open your mind to him. You, also, may have the mind of Christ.)

As you learn to love prayer, you will crave more time for it.

Extend your fixed periods of prayer when you can, but remember that every day will offer you unexpected moments.

Don't waste them.

They are tiny grains that can be turned by God to gold.

Every morning, remember that they will come.

Be ready to take them.

You, also, can make time.

34

HOW TO USE THE TIME WE GET

THE cutting out (or cutting down) of unnecessary things in our lives and the wise economy of odd moments will be meaningless if we do not clearly understand what use we can make of the time we have saved. Prayer and meditation are always and everywhere possible. There are other wise uses we can make of those salvaged moments as well.

It is often in the odd moments of the day that the termites of negativism and depression get into our minds. We all have daily mechanical tasks to do which have become so habitual that we can do them with efficiency—and at the same time think of something else: the husband driving his car, the wife doing her housework, the policeman walking his beat, and the miner hewing the coal. In the days when I was an accountant, I could add up columns of figures for hours, do it with accuracy, and simultaneously think of something else. The figures just added themselves up in one part of my mind.

Moreover, there are odd minutes in all our days when we are not thinking of anything in particular: as we sit in a bus or train, wait to be served in a restaurant or shop, dress in the morning and undress at night . . . .

What is our mind doing when it is not doing anything in particular? It is certainly not blank—not even in our sleeping—but (moved sometimes by fear and sometimes by wish) it indulges in what the psychologist calls "fantasy thinking" and the man in the street describes as "a daydream." Odd images flit across the mind. A person is the chief actor in all kinds of little mental dramas or escapades. Strange things float up from the lower strata of the mind, and if a psychologist could examine the stuff of our daydreams, there would be few mysteries about us.

It is in this realm of our fantasy thinking that our fears and desires have a way of disclosing themselves and, by filling the mind with foreboding, often pull us down to the things we dread. Few things in our life come nearer to revealing our real selves than our daydreams, and in few areas of our lives could we find more help in reaching the ends we seek. Many people, if questioned, would have to admit that at such times their minds are assailed (and sometimes completely held) by thoughts of fear and defeat; of ill health and failure; of grave worries concerning themselves and their dear ones; of sickness, accident, death, and disgrace. More people are suffering from scarecoma than glaucoma, from fearosis than cillosis, from apprehendicitis than appendicitis.

The author of the Song of Songs speaks of the little foxes which spoil the vineyards, and there are also little apprehensions which constantly visit our minds and interlard our talk. "I shall be late! . . ." "I shall get into trouble! . . ." "I fear it will rain! . . ." "Just my luck! . . ." "Things always turn out this way for me. . . ."

We need to take a positive and fighting attitude toward all these apprehensions—large and small. Does your mind run on those lines? Do you catch yourself thinking those dark thoughts—and expressing those little whines?

Answer them! Recognize each of those fantasy fears the moment it comes and replace it with the opposite. Every believer in the Christian God knows that God is Love and that he himself is the object of God's special care. Affirm the truth to yourself.

> No harm from Him can come to me
> On ocean or on shore.

If he permits what appears to be a disaster to overtake you, there must be the possibility of great good as its fruit—or he would never have allowed it. Affirm, therefore, in the face of the ugly thing: "I declare this thing to be good unto me!" Nourish in yourself trust in God. Do it by the way of affirmation. Never let your mind wallow in fear and negation. Quietly, resolutely, and confidently, replace it with an affirmation of the truth. Hold the affirmation in mind as long as you can. When it sinks to the unconscious, it will sink "with healing in its wings." (A.S.V., R.S.V.) A subconscious stored with such treasures makes any one of us a wealthy man.

Cut out all those *little* expressions of apprehension too. Not a whine as you say, "Things always turn out this way for me . . . ," but a smile as you affirm, "All things work together for good to them that love God!" Your God is a loving Father and all things are in his hands.

But it is not only with our thoughts that we can work in these less-occupied moments of our day. We can work with our feelings too.

We have recognized that the New Testament gives us a picture of the world surrounded by the love and power of God, with the power waiting to pour in through any faithful mind and the love waiting to flow through any dedicated heart.

Everybody living a busy life in the world touches other lives every day. Some people touch scores of lives in a day. The contact may be brief, but so potent is the love of God that the briefest contact can impart some awareness of it. It easily travels on a word. It can move in a smile. A *thought* can convey it.

What a difference can be felt in a railway carriage, or in the depression of a doctor's waiting-room, if one person arrives who is a channel of the love of God. It is not necessary to *talk*. Expression and demeanor disclose it. Thinking, in turn, of the people about you and loving them at the same time does something for their spirit which words cannot describe.

I remember a lady's telling me many years ago that it was her practice to offer herself to God as a channel of his love for all the people with whom she traveled—strangers, usually, to her and with whom she would probably exchange no word at all. But to each in turn, she would direct her thought and seek to canalize the stream of God's love.

She smiled as she told me. "I sometimes feel," she said, "that I have in my hands the nozzle of a great love and, each in turn, I pour the love of God over them."

I entertain little doubt that the people involved in these brief encounters were unconsciously helped by this good woman's silent ministries, but I am quite positive that she herself was a radiant Christian. You cannot be offering yourself all the time as a channel of God's love without gaining from it yourself. A strange charm was imparted to the channel through which that holy love was swift to flow.

Is there something here to copy? The simple revivalists of the nineteenth century had a hymn in which they implored the Almighty to make them "a channel of blessing today." Here is a method to help God answer that prayer. Think of yourself that way. Be joined in heart to the vast reservoir of infinite love and silently direct the stream to all with whom you come in contact. Turn it to your fellow travelers. Turn it toward those with whom you live and those with whom you work. Your aim is to help them, but no one eager to help others fails to get help himself. If nothing else, the spirit of positive love flowing through you is a solid barrier built against fear and negativism, and the dangerous trickle of depression will never be able to percolate through.

Finally, I suggest as yet another way of directing your thoughts in the odd moments as they come, that you have in the antechamber of your mind "a word for the day"—a different word for each day of the week, a word easily summoned and rich in its power to relate you to God.

Here is a way I have found helpful myself and have taught to other people.

There are seven days in the week. Let us take seven of the facets of Christ's mind which have drawn us in this study (and which are set down in the New Testament as fruit of the Holy Spirit as well) and put them in an order most easily remembered. Let us take Love, Joy, Peace, Endurance, Kindness, Faithfulness, and Self-control. Let us change the words (though not the sense) and put those seven facets of Christ's mind in alphabetical order. Let Affection stand for Love, and Benevolence for Kindness, and Calmness for Peace, and Discipline for Self-control. Endurance and Faithfulness fit into the pattern of themselves, and Gladness can take the place of Joy. Link each word to a day in the week and remember the word with every morning as it comes.

On Sunday	it is	Affection
On Monday	it is	Benevolence
On Tuesday	it is	Calmness
On Wednesday	it is	Discipline
On Thursday	it is	Endurance
On Friday	it is	Faithfulness
On Saturday	it is	Gladness

In any odd moment of the day, think of the key word. Instead of fretting and fuming at unexpected obstructions, turn your mind to "the word for the day." Instead of indulging those foolish and sometimes dangerous daydreams, take the word out of your memory and turn it over on your tongue. Say it to yourself. Say it loud enough to hear it. Hold the *sense* of it in your mind as you say it.

Affection—the limitless love of God, which is ready to course through me to other people.

Benevolence—which is that same love, active as kindness in the briefer contacts of life.

Calmness—the peace of God, surpassing understanding but ready to rule in the heart.

Discipline—the power God gives to control all the impulses of nature and make them serve his ends.

Endurance—the courage of Christ to persist in all things good and never to give in to evil.

Faithfulness—the central loyalty of the soul to God, whatever the cost.

Gladness—the inward happiness of those who believe, sometimes bubbling into exuberance and sometimes glowing with deep content.

Each of the words grows richer with use. It absorbs something of the spirit of every meditation upon it. It deepens the quality it names.

Say it. Savor it. See yourself with it. With your mind open to God and all your soul lost in this high covetousness, draw your Master's nature into your own. Recognize, indeed, that it is already coming in. Exult in it. This is the supreme end of our quest—Christ in us, the bliss of earth and greater bliss of heaven.

It cannot be kept selfishly—even with selfishness in its most "refined" form. It is not the *mind of Christ* unless it is passing through you to others. It cannot end in ecstatic states of mind. If it is the mind of the Master, it will lead us to service and to some kind of sacrifice.

In a life so lived, no moments are wasted. As we become aware of our need of other facets of his mind, we can make other sets of daily words. (I have used, many times, every letter in the alphabet but X!) Prayer and the various meditations I have commended will all help. So our stubborn natures will be changed. So the mind of Christ will come in. So he will answer our prayer:

Heavenly Adam, Life divine,
Change my nature into Thine;
Move and spread throughout my soul,
Actuate and fill the whole;
Be it I no longer now
Living in the flesh, but Thou.

Meditation XII

With most meditations, we choose the time and seek the quiet, but in this "Cult of the Salvaged Moment" we cannot choose the time or seek the quiet.

These moments come as they will and often in noisy places.

> Around us rolls the ceaseless tide
> Of business, toil, and care.

The quiet must be in our soul. We have to withdraw within, and God will meet us. Our one piece of preparation is to know what we will do when the moments come.

Never indulge in negative thinking.

The moment you are aware of it within you, replace it with healthy, confident, God-directed thought.

Look upon every contact of the day (however brief) as opportunity. It is not your business to "push" religion at people. That often gets religion a bad name. Speak only as God directs you. But learn to have your heart as an open channel of Christ's love. Look on people (as George Fox always tried to do) "in the love of God." The love will reach them—though you may not say a word.

Make a set of key words, taken from the heart of religion and easily remembered, and link each one of them to a day. Enrich them by prayerful meditation on their central meaning. Have them always on call. In any moment, place them in the center of your thinking . . . Power, Peace, Fullness, Freedom, Love, Life. . . .

Murmur to Christ:

> Thou art wisdom, power, and love,
> *And all Thou art is mine.*

A PRAYER FOR THE DIVINE INDWELLING

Lord Jesus, I am longing
  From sin to be set free:
To find my deep desiring
  Forever fixed on Thee.
All hope I now abandon
  Myself to conquer sin;
Invade my willing nature
  And come and dwell within.

The passing years oppress me,
  My growth in grace so slow:
My wayward fickle cravings
  Have leagued me to the foe,
Myself to self disloyal,
  I loathe yet love my sin:
Now hear my heartfelt pleading
  And come and dwell within.

If Thou should'st stand close by me
  'Tis more than I deserve;
But, being still outside me,
  From virtue, yet, I swerve.
Come nearer, Lord, than near me,
  My succour to begin:
Usurp the heart that craves Thee!
  O come and dwell within.